D1097864

"THE WORLD IS MY PARISH"
THE METHODISTS
ARE ONE PEOPLE
THE METHODIST CHURCH
1939

Frontier Bishop

Frontier Bishop

The Life and Times of Robert Richford Roberts

WORTH MARION TIPPY

NEW YORK ABINGDON PRESS NASHVILLE

FRONTIER BISHOP

Library of Congress Catalog Card Number: 58-5394

SET UP, PRINTED, AND BOUND BY THE PARTHENON PRESS, AT NASHVILLE, TENNESSEE, UNITED STATES OF AMERICA

TO

RUSSELL J. HUMBERT

President of DePauw University

Preface

ON THE CAMPUS OF DEPAUW UNIVERSITY THERE IS A GRAVE which generations of students have passed between classes, little knowing the romantic story of the man who lies buried beneath its marble shaft. The beloved woman who shared his incredible labors and hardships lies beside him. It is the grave of Bishop Roberts and his wife, Elizabeth Oldham. He was buried there on January 19, 1844. Fifteen years later, fifteen lonely years, she was laid beside him. Such marks of affection and honor, such a burial place on the grounds of a seat of learning, were seldom granted to men of his time.

Robert Richford Roberts was the sixth bishop of the Methodist Episcopal Church. He was born in Maryland in 1778 and died at Lawrenceport, Indiana, in 1843. He was consecrated a bishop on May 16, 1816. He was thirty-eight at the time, one of the youngest men to be elevated to that distinction. This was only fourteen years after he had come from the frontier of western Pennsylvania to be admitted on trial to the Baltimore Conference. He had come in homespun with the stamp of the wild upon him; but his tall strong body, his impressive countenance, his youthful freshness and vigor had challenged the attention of the Conference.

The church was by then well started on its way to its extraordinary career in the New World. It had weathered the storm of the Revolution, and, like the nation, had freed itself from the control of the mother country. The memorable Christmas Conference of 1784 had definitely, and with rare wisdom and unanimity, devised an organization for the new church—an organization suited to the conditions and expanding frontiers of the nation.

Roberts had nothing to do with these first memorable undertakings, but he was soon to have a major part in their developments. He was a child of six at the time of the Christmas Conference. He grew into manhood during the early years, when the foundations of the church were being laid. By the time of his consecration the exceptional men, the great humble men who were its leaders, were growing old or had died. Thomas Coke and Thomas Vasey had gone back to England. Valiant Francis Asbury had just died, as had Jesse Lee and Freeborn Garrettson. William McKendree, the stalwart Tennessean, badly broken, was the only bishop left when Enoch George and Roberts were elected.

Roberts had known the founders in their days of power. Asbury and Coke had ordained him. He had met with them for fourteen years in the sessions of the Baltimore Conference and in four General Conferences. Asbury had given him special attention; and finally Asbury's mantle fell upon him.

Roberts was the frontiersman to the day of his death. Although he became one of the foremost religious leaders of his time, he was still the adventurer in a new country. In his youth he had hunted and trapped like the fur hunters of the North. Before he became of age, he had cleared land and built his own log cabin in the wilderness of the Shenango Valley. He was helping clear ground in Indiana four months before he died. Long after he became a bishop he liked to follow deer in the forest. When he was free, being now a bishop, to live where he chose, he established his episcopal residence in what was then wilderness of the hill country of southern Indiana. Here, in utmost seclusion, he lived for the next quarter century, at first under most primitive conditions. From this isolated place he left on horseback on his amazing episcopal journeys to all parts of the nation, returning after long absences to work on his lands.

Bishop Roberts came to Indiana on the crest of the wave of population which swept over the Appalachian Mountains at the opening of the nineteenth century. There has been nothing since on this continent so vast, so spectacular, so moving, unless it be the gold rush to California or the saga of the Oregon Trail. The bishop must be seen against the background of that great migration. He was one with it from his seventh year, when his family moved to the then frontier of western Pennsylvania, until his death in 1843. No man of his time experienced more of its hardships and adventures, or traveled more widely, or better understood the migrants, or was better prepared for the leadership which came to him so early in life.

Roberts kept no journal and has left few records of his fascinating life. There remain only texts and fragments of sermons, excerpts from correspondence preserved by Charles Elliott in his life of Roberts, descriptions by contemporaries, and references in Minutes of the conferences. What a contribution he might have made to the history of the Mississippi Valley had he kept a journal!

His leading biographers, Charles Elliott, Matthew Simpson, and William Clark Larrabee, had known him long and intimately. The bishop had ordained Elliott and Simpson. Each of the three had access to a manuscript dictated to Simpson by Roberts while his portrait was being painted for Indiana Asbury University in 1842. The manuscript covers the earlier period from 1778 to 1808, but it is condensed and often loosely written. Simpson used it for a brief biography and for the article on Roberts in the *Cyclopaedia of Methodism.*

I have endeavored to limit the use of footnotes in deference to the general reader, using them only when it seemed necessary. Another and more debatable departure is the occasional use of conversations to enliven and give a feeling of reality and continuity to the factual narrative. I may say that I have been guided in writing these brief passages by fragments of conversation preserved in the Simpson manuscript, and in the Elliott biography, quoted, I think, from Mrs. Roberts. I have lived so long with the Robertses during the writing of this book that I seem to know how they talked.

I am indebted to DePauw University and to many persons for assistance in library and field research: especially to Mrs. Vera Southwick Cooper, librarian at DePauw University; and to William H. Andrews of Lawrenceport who often took me about the Lawrenceport countryside. Frank McIntire owns the original Roberts' farm near Lawrenceport. He helped his father tear down the big log house built in 1822, and therefore saw it as it was. Mrs. B. F. Johnson, who lives near Orleans, Indiana, and is a descendant of the bishop's niece Esther, has important memorabilia from the Roberts' home—including rare portraits—and gave me traditions concerning the family. The memorabilia are in the archives at Greencastle.

Mrs. John Stevenson of Sharon, Pennsylvania, a descendant of William and Elizabeth Lindsey, took me to the Roberts' farm and the mill site in the valley of the Little Shenango River where Roberts came in 1796 as a young man of eighteen. Virgil Johnson of Mercer, Pennsylvania, genealogist of the Roberts family and a descendant of Elizabeth Lindsey, helped me generously. To these persons, to Mr. and Mrs. Ray M. Walker of Laurel, Mississippi, to Evelyn Craig of Vevay, Indiana, who joined in the search in Indiana, and to many others, my grateful thanks.

Contents

Chapter I

Childhood in Maryland

IT WAS MIDSUMMER, PRECISELY AUGUST 2, 1778, WHEN ROBERT Richford Roberts was born. The place was a little farm in Frederick County, Maryland. "God's Gift" they had named it, as if the fertile soil were a heavenly benefaction.

Central Maryland is a lovely country; a land of rolling hills, rich valleys, and the ranges of the Blue Ridge Mountains to the west. Cotoctin Mountain, gorgeous in October, rose back of the place where young Robert played with his brothers and sisters. It was lit in the morning by the sun from over the eastern hills, and lay against the sky at sunset. Storms came sweeping over the valley, and in winter snow sifted down upon the pine trees. Chestnuts fell on the grass when early frosts opened their burs. The peace of the mountain, the wonder of earth and sky, and the love of God sank unawares into the child's mind, to appear later in a soul like that of St. Francis.

But while the child opened his eyes on beauty, he was also born into the turmoil of war. Robert Morgan Roberts, his father, was in the army of George Washington. The farm lay but a little west of the marching armies. The Revolutionary War was in its third year, and was to drag on five more weary years before peace came to the distracted and impoverished colonies. The battles of Long Island, White Plains, and Brandywine had been fought and lost. Washington had barely escaped disaster at Germantown, but had won at Princeton and Trenton.

Robert Morgan Roberts is a shadowy figure through the mists to time. He had battle experience at White Plains and Brandywine, fought under LaFayette, and was probably at Valley Forge during the bitter winter of 1777-78. He vanishes in the Shenango Valley at the dawn of the century, but he held the respect and affection of his children. He was tall and strong like his son, was deeply religious, and had the carriage of a soldier. Bishop Roberts described his father as, "remarkable for his gentleness and kindness of nature, and upright in his conduct to all men." [1]

Mary Richford, Robert's mother, had married at sixteen. She was the only child of Thomas and Esther Richford. They came from the Eastern Shore of Maryland, where the Roberts had originally settled. She was given some educational advantages, for it was she who taught the children. As described to Simpson by her son, "She was of low statue, was active and buoyant, and was lively in her disposition." [2] As a girl she liked to sing and dance, as did her children.

Robert Morgan Roberts' father was a well-to-do farmer, but by the Maryland law of primogeniture his lands went to the oldest son. Robert Morgan was therefore on his own when he came back from the war. By 1777 his wife had given birth to eight children. Two boys died, one from dysentery, the other a tragic death by drowning in the spring near the house. Each of these boys successively had been named Robert after their father. Three of the children—Mary, Thomas, and Elizabeth—were triplets. The mother was carrying Robert, the third to be named after the father, during the winter of 1777-78. While her husband was at the front, the management of the farm and the care of the children, and finally the trials of expectant motherhood fell upon her

[1] From an unpublished manuscript by Matthew Simpson. The original of this manuscript is in the Library of Congress and a photostat is in the Archives at DePauw University. This quotation appears on p. 1.

[2] *Ibid.*

valiant shoulders. She was no longer the vivacious girl who loved to sing and dance.

The parents had done what they could for the education of their children, but there was little opportunity. The mother began to teach Robert to read when he was four, and he was sent to school for a year before the family left Maryland for the frontier. By the time he was seven he could read the Bible "very intelligently," revealing a quick mind and a gift of memory. But after the family left Maryland, formal education came to an end for many years.

However, other educational influences of great importance were shaping the young child's mind. He had the good fortune to have older and younger brothers and sisters, so that he had never to play alone and was not a spoiled child. He learned the skills of a farm by doing. He grew up in the community of a large family; in this case, a family singularly devoted to one another and refined by its strong loyalties.

But of greater importance than these advantages was the spiritual inheritance he received from his parents. They were communicants of the Church of England in Maryland. The father was a zealous churchman, the mother instinctively religious. One may infer from Robert's devotion to his mother that he was the child of her spiritual longings. Family worship, using the Prayer Book, had been maintained in the home long before they went into the wilderness.

The family were communicants of All Souls Church in Frederick, one of the few Church of England parishes in Maryland to maintain services during the Revolution, most rectors being suspected of loyalty to the mother country. The Roberts children learned the catechism. Its classic sentences, like hymns learned in childhood, lay deep in Robert's mind, to influence his later thinking and attitudes. He knew the Prayer Book and always felt at home in the services of the church of his childhood.

The same beliefs and religious customs were continued for several years when the family moved to Ligonier. The rector in Maryland had cautioned the parents to guard the children against the sects which were springing up on the frontier. Robert Morgan took the admonition seriously, and the children shared his feeling. When the older children were converted under the ardent preaching of Methodist itinerants on the Redstone circuit, the elder Roberts kept aloof, and the son held with his father.

It is evident that Robert's early life rested deeply on Church of England foundations. This was also the case with Asbury, Coke, and Whatcoat and supremely so with Wesley. The first six bishops of the Methodist Church were Church of England men. Wesley never abandoned the mother church, but sought to the last to persuade the Bishop of London, who had supervision of the churches in the colonies, to authorize his clergy to provide the sacraments for the Methodist societies. What might have happened had he done so is an interesting but fruitless speculation. Perhaps it is as well for what the church had to do in the New World that the petitions were never granted.

In Roberts' later years as an itinerant preacher and finally as a bishop his background in the Church of England was a permanent influence. It contributed to his singular dignity, self-control, and orderliness. Methodism brought him a mystical experience, zeal, and emotional release. The combination gave him freedom and power.

Chapter II

The Pennsylvania Frontier

WHEN THE CHILD ROBERT WAS SEVEN, HIS FATHER SOLD HIS farm in Maryland and moved to western Pennsylvania. He had secured four hundred acres of land in the Ligonier Valley fifty miles east of Pittsburgh, probably as a soldier of the Revolution.

That part of Pennsylvania was then on the frontier. It was safe from Indians, but the memory of massacres was still fresh in the minds of settlers. The public domain had not as yet been transferred by the states to the central government, and Pennsylvania was offering land at low cost to attract settlers. The tide of migration into the Ohio Valley was to wait another twenty years, although it had already begun into Kentucky. The movement of population westward had almost stopped during the Revolution, but was beginning again into the nearer valleys of the Allegheny Mountains.

Robert Morgan Roberts had little capital, but he had initiative and courage and was quick to take advantage of the opportunity. The war had just ended, and his discharge was recent when he acted. One may be sure that he and his wife did not take the step without misgivings. It is not easy to tear up roots from a place where one has lived for many years; and they were sobered when they thought of their ten children, including Priscilla, two, and Nancy, six months. The distance over the mountains does not seem formidable today, but it was a long journey in 1785. However, they were driven by necessity, and a rainbow shone in the western sky.

Roberts had first to make a trip to the Ligonier to locate land, and then a second trip to build a cabin and clear enough ground for a garden and a field of corn. He had helped his brother Thomas when he had homesteaded near Bedford, and Thomas in turn helped him build his cabin and clear a plot of ground. A field of corn and a garden were imperative to carry them over the first winter. They could not take enough with them for so large a family, and supplies at Fort Ligonier were too costly for their slender means.

When the work was finished, he hurried back to Maryland to bring his family. August days were lengthening, and it was necessary to return before winter set in. What excitement when he rode into the family yard at "God's Gift." The children crowded about him, all talking at once, asking about the new home, eager to tell him what had happened while he had been away. When he found that they were well, and had learned from John that the crops were in, he knew they were ready. Supper over and the children gone to bed, he and Mary talked long into the night.

They had choice of two roads to Ligonier—the old Cumberland or Braddock Road, which passed through Frederick from Baltimore to Pittsburgh and the West; or the newer Forbes Road, route of the 1758 expedition against Fort Duquesne, which led directly from Carlisle to Bedford, Fort Ligonier, and Pittsburgh. The Cumberland Road had been neglected after the building of the northern route to the West, so Roberts took the Forbes Road. It passed within a mile of his land at Fort Ligonier. Both highways were primitive at best—narrow, ungraded, obstructed by rocks and tree stumps.

At last the morning came when they were to say good-by to Maryland. Friends and relatives came to see them off. Everything they could possibly carry had been loaded on the wagon: household goods and clothing; tools and spare parts for building and farming; precious seeds for planting; food for the journey and the first months at Ligonier: the family Bible and their few books; some prized treasures of the children. The stock was driven by the older children; and except for the mother and smaller children, the family walked.

We can follow, in imagination, the little caravan of the Roberts family as it moved slowly along this highway. The first part of the journey was through fairly settled country, some of which they knew. As they advanced, the road began to climb. Progress was slow because of the stock. The children were kept running after them, for the animals were always hungry and stopped to browse at every opportunity. The season was advancing into October, and the mountainsides were in brilliant colors. Evenings were cold and the morning air crisp, but the members of the family were warmly clad and were used to life in the open. There was little rain at that time of year, and the early snows had not begun. The journey might seem formidable to one who has never lived on a frontier, but to Roberts it was like soldiering; and to the children, an exciting adventure. To the mother and her babies it was wearisome and exhausting.

The best times were the evenings about the campfire. They were drawn together by the darkness and fascinated by the flames. The fire shone on their faces and silhouetted the trees which closed in about them. They sang together after the custom of their Welsh forbears. The children begged their father for stories about the war—about Washington, LaFayette, and the young French officers; about Valley Forge and the eastern cities which he had seen in his soldiering. They asked about the new home and Indians and fierce wild creatures in the forest around them. These stories made their flesh creep, but they loved them.

Sleeping in a tent was an old experience to the father, but new and exciting to the children. They had loved make-believe tents of old blankets, but now they were sleeping in a real tent. Robert and four-year-old Lewis lay close together under their comforter, listening to the sound of the night wind in the pines, the crash of a falling tree, and the distant baying of a wolf and the answering call of its mate—fearful to their childish imaginations.

All journeys come to an end, even life itself. The day is done, the journey ended, the project accomplished. A night came when the Roberts made their last camp, sat about their last campfire, slept their last night in the white tent. Toward noon the next day they climbed the pass over Chestnut Ridge and entered the Ligonier Valley. When they reached the floor of the valley, they found themselves in the midst of towering hills.

Fort Ligonier lay at the center of the valley. It was a typical frontier military post surrounded by a stockade enclosing two or three acres of ground, with cleared space on all sides reaching beyond rifle range. Within were barracks, storage for munitions and supplies, and a space for settlers in time of danger from Indians.

After a brief stop near the fort the family moved on to their land. It lay five miles to the southwest and less than a mile south of the Forbes Road where it began the ascent of Laurel Ridge. The present Lincoln Highway passes a mile north of the original road. They reached the new cabin toward noon. It lay nestled among trees at the foot of a wooded ridge. A spring, so indispensable to the frontier home, flowed out of the rock back of the cabin. The little valley was shut in by ridges. The farm extended south for a mile along a stream. The western line lay along the foot of Laurel Ridge.

One dwells upon the setting of the farm because the child Robert was to live among these hills for the next eleven impressionable years. Here he learned the discipline of work, the experience of hardship, and the strong loyalties of a closely knit family. Here he found the woman he loved. Here his creative mind, chafing against limitations, determined to achieve independence. Here he became aware of the presence of God and heard the call to the sacred vocation to which he gave his life.

Let us look at this family as they sat talking after the first supper in the wilderness cabin, the firelight glowing on their faces. They were a happy group, singularly knit together in affecton and loyalty. John ("old Sobersides" they called him) was twenty-two. In gaiety Sarah, eighteen, was like her mother. The triplets—Thomas, Mary, and Elizabeth—were fourteen, Esther, nine. Robert was seven and Lewis four. These two were inseparable playmates, and later carried their intimacy into far-off Indiana. The little girls were the joy of the family. The parents were fortunate, both in the characters of their children, and because the mother had dependable assistance in the home and the father on the farm. They were spending their first night in a sparsely settled county surrounded by immense forests, with no near neighbors, no friendly church, no school; but there were so many of them that they formed a community by themselves.

The family awakened next morning at daybreak. They were so packed together, the twelve of them, that no one could get up without awakening the rest. They were also accustomed to early bedtime and early rising; and who could sleep on such a morning, the first in the new home?

The father got up first, uncovered live coals from the ashes, and started a fire against the backlog. The warmth was gratifying in the crisp air and the flames cheerful and companionable. Soon the entire family was astir. John and Tom went out to look after the stock and to bring water from the spring. The girls set about getting breakfast and helping their mother with the younger children. Robert and Lewis, who slept together, awakened dreamily, thinking themselves in the familiar home in Maryland, and then, realizing, jumped out of bed excitedly and climbed down the ladder into the living room.

There was reason for urgency. They had come on a long journey, like Abraham gone into a far country. Everything was strange and adventurous. Winter was approaching and the cabin had yet to be made snug for the cold months. The stock must be sheltered and food accumulated for the family and the animals. Food was always a problem for so large a family on the frontier, and was doubly so for the stock over the first winter. The house was as yet wanting the simplest furniture. There was everything to do and everything was needed at once. The girls had hastily made beds on the floor for the first night, and things were scattered about. They had now to make the house livable and to settle down to the routine of life and work in this formidable wilderness.

Robert Morgan went out into the yard while breakfast was being prepared and walked about with John and Thomas, planning the day. As they stood talking, their eyes rested on the dense woods crowding close about them. Huge trees, centuries old, must be cut down and burned to make way for fields, a herculean task for men working only with axe and wedge and fire.

"It's a big job," he said at last. "We must get at it soon. We must clear another field during the winter in time for spring planting." But observing a look on the boys' faces, he added, "Don't be discouraged. We shall do it a field at a time."

Sarah called them to breakfast, and they joined the circle about the fireplace. They sat about in little groups, each with his own plate, for there was as yet no common table. They did not eat in silence as was usual in frontier homes. Theirs was a gay and friendly family. The room was filled with the chatter and laughter of the children.

Breakfast over, they went to work with zest. The mother told the men what she wanted them to do. Would they please set up the big iron kettle in the yard and heat water for the washing? Would one of them hang a line between trees for the wash? Would they drive pegs into the walls of the cabin so that she could hang garments? "We can wait a little for beds and a table," she told them.

Even Robert and Lewis wanted to help. They were told to go to the garden, to gather the potatoes as they were dug, and to spread them in the sun to dry. This gave them a feeling of importance. They liked to see the clusters of potatoes lifted from the ground, and shouted when a large one came up with the fork. They were given the job of pulling the onions and turnips and gathering them into heaps.

The cabin had no cellar for storage, and there was not time to build a dugout in the yard, so Robert did the next best thing. He dug shallow holes in the ground, three or four feet in width, and lined them thickly with leaves. When the potatoes were dry, they were piled in conical heaps, covered with leaves, and over the leaves was placed a thick layer of earth. Here they kept safely through the long winter.

When the men came in for supper at nightfall, they found that the women had finished their work. On a sheet lay freshly washed linen in neatly sprinkled rolls, ready for ironing, and the girls had supper waiting.

The meal over, the family lingered talking in little groups about the fire, the parents sitting apart in quiet conversation. Suddenly Tom caught some words his mother was saying: "I think, Robert, you will have to try to get some fresh meat. We are using too much of the reserve stock we brought from Maryland. Don't you think you could get a wild turkey or even a deer in time for Sunday? There must be game in the woods about us. I know you are pressed for time, but we could wait a little longer for the things you have to make for the house."

Before his father could answer, Tom broke in, "Oh, father! Please let John and me take the rifle and go for a deer. We saw one the day we came here. I am sure we could get one."

By now all were listening. The mother interposed, "But,

Robert, I didn't mean that you should send the boys. Do you think it safe for them to go alone with the rifle into the big woods?"

The father answered, "I think we can trust them, mother. They must learn their way in the woods and also the habits of the wildlife around us. John knows how to handle a gun safely. We shall have to depend for a long time on the rifle for meat."

Then to the boys, "You may take the day off tomorrow and start as early as you like. The earlier the better, for the deer are feeding in the morning."

Before they broke up for the night, Robert took down the Prayer Book and read a passage of Scripture and a prayer from one of the services which could be used in families. Then they sang a hymn. It was the routine by which the father kept alive the customs of their church and the spirit of religion in the home.

At early dawn next morning John and Tom entered the woods. They came back at night with a deer. The dog saw them first and came barking furiously, but seeing the deer, sniffed at it suspiciously. At the sound of the dog the family hurried out of the house. They had become increasingly anxious as the day advanced. The boys were tired and hungry, so the father took over care of the deer while the mother hurried supper.

The bringing in of the first deer was an event of importance as well as excitement. Henceforth their main dependence for meat was on the forest. Wild geese, turkeys, ducks, pheasants, and squirrels became welcome variations in diet. The woods about them furnished chestnuts for dressing, and wild plums and berries in abundance, until an orchard could be grown. The vital importance of meat gave justification to the excitement of hunting. The father let the boys go freely, indeed would send them whenever they could be spared. Curing, or "jerking," venison over a fire became a major activity at the farm. The frontier witnessed a partial return of the hunting stage of society, and hunting became the favorite recreation of the men. Robert and Lewis were too young to carry a rifle, but they were greatly excited. Robert was later to become the most skillful hunter of them all, but apparently he did not hunt in his early youth. The older boys took it upon themselves.

The day following the hunt was Saturday. The father and John dressed the deer and began the preparation of the hide, while Robert and Lewis watched the process. It was fastened against one side of the cabin in the sun for scraping and rubbing with salt and fat, after the way of Indians. It came out soft and pliable, suitable for garments and thongs of buckskin, incredibly strong for mending harness and tying packs on horses.

Weekly baths on Saturday afternoons were a problem. In the warm months the men preferred to go to the creek, but in cold weather all must bathe in the house, using the washtub. Twelve baths, water carried from the spring, hot water from the big iron kettle in the yard, four unwilling youngsters to be scrubbed! To carry the water and keep it hot was Tom's job. To keep the schedule going fell to the mother.

Sunday was looked forward to by the entire family. They observed the day religiously with relaxation from all but necessary work. The father and mother had a welcome time to themselves, and the children were free to do as they liked within the accepted sanctity of the day. Robert and Lewis played together. The older children took a long walk in the woods. It was the girls' first chance to explore the neighborhood. Letters were written to old friends in Maryland.

But the event of the day was the venison dinner. The roast was set simmering in the Dutch oven in the early morning and potatoes were added toward noon. The mother brought out delicacies she had hoarded from the old home. Corn bread freshly baked in a skillet, of which they never tired, was served with maple syrup, which the children liked with the bread. They sat for the first time about a long table which had been completed during the week. Robert Morgan had cut down a popular tree, and he and John had split and hewed puncheon boards, fastened them at the ends with hickory pegs, and smoothed down the surface with an adz.

When evening came and they sat about the fireplace, the father read a service from the Prayer Book, and the family joined in the familiar responses. They sang hymns of the church, such as Addison's, "When All Thy Mercies, O My God," and songs of the Revolution. What a picture, could their friends in Maryland have looked in upon them!

Chapter III

Youth in the Ligonier Valley

THE WEEKS WHICH FOLLOWED WERE DEVOTED TO BUILDING—the father, John, and Thomas working together. They first erected a crude log shelter for the stock, by its side a shed for wagon and tools, a stockade, and nearby a crib for the precious stock of corn. The cabin was banked with earth to keep out the cold winds of winter from under the floor.

These essentials completed, they turned to the house, and began construction of beds for the family. These were built against the walls of the cabin. The men had no nails and worked only with axe, broad axe, adz, augers, and hickory pins. Flattened poles, rounded at the ends, were driven into holes bored into the logs, and rested at the other ends on legs forced tightly into auger holes. Straight poles, smoothed with the adz and notched at the ends, were laid on either side and across them wide puncheon boards from poplar trees. On these were laid mattresses filled with husks from the corn. The Robertses had brought bed linen, quilts, and comforters from the home in Maryland.

The men also laid shelving on pins driven into the logs, and a mantle over the fireplace above which the rifle was hung. When it was finished, the house was comfortable and had a rugged beauty.

The men then turned to clearing land. Snow had fallen, and the woods lay about them. They selected a tract of the richest ground and the one most easily cultivated. A scene followed which has vanished from American life. Magnificent trees, centuries old, fabulously valuable if standing today, but then a formidable obstacle, had to be cut down and burned in order to make way for fields. There was nothing else to do. Forests had been growing and dying, devastated by wind and fire and insect life, with incredible waste from countless ages. Such is the prodigality of Nature. Another forest has matured since then and others will continue to grow.

The men first girdled the big trees with their axes. Cut off from the flow of life-giving sap, they would never leaf again. Smaller trees were cut down and dragged into rows for burning. Then fire, Lanier's "Workman Heat," began its deadly work. Women at the house heard the sharp crack of the axes and the crash of falling timber. Bushes were grubbed from their roots, piled on the logs, and set afire. The surrounding woods and the night were lit by flames. Roberts did not attempt to dig out the stumps or to cut down the large trees. He plowed or dug around them the first years and left the roots to rot in the ground. The deadened trees were cut down the third season and the field finally cleared of obstructions.

When spring finally came to the valley, Roberts planted an orchard of apple, cherry, pear, and plum trees, a larger garden, and fields of corn and flax. He needed more acreage, but none could be available until the next winter's clearing. The stock had to browse upon foliage and wild peas until a meadow could be started. They were fed enough corn to keep them strong. To make garments for the family the women required flax for spinning and weaving. The time of sheep and wool had not yet come to the valley.

The years which followed passed in much the same way, except that the children were growing up. The acreage of cleared land steadily increased, and the standard of living rose. The valley was filling with settlers, and the young people at the Roberts' home soon had friends. There was social dancing in the cabin and in neighbor's homes, and the older children thought little of walking miles to these parties.

Life in the valley was salutary except for two vital deficiencies. During the first years there was no school and no church. Schools came in time, but too late for the first generation of children. When the schools did come, they were private ones, held at first in settlers' cabins and taught by itinerant teachers who were paid by subscription. In the Roberts family were six bright children of school age, ranging from Lewis, five, to the triplets, fourteen. The religious life of the children was cared for in the home, but formal education was neglected, apparently without much concern.

These years witnessed a rapid development in the child Robert's life. He came to Ligonier a child of seven; at fourteen he was an overgrown awkward boy, careless in dress and slow of movement. At sixteen he looked like a man. At eighteen he was fully grown.

All during adolescence he was careless about dress. He worked about the farm like a laborer. "His clothing," says Elliott, "was the common back-woods costume: the broad rimmed, low crowned, white wool hat, the hunting shirt of tow linen, buck-skin breaches, and moccasins or coarse shoes." [1] He dressed so on all occasions, unconscious of his appearance—or indifferent. When people came to the cabin to meetings, especially quarterly meetings to which they assembled from the entire circuit, he looked after their horses as if he were a hired man. This was natural to him and seemed the thing to do, but to dress so roughly on such occasions was noticed. The family must have talked to him about it, but without avail. Probably he knew too well the limited resources of his father and would not ask for money to buy Sunday clothes. Anyway, he didn't greatly care. He was thus about dress all his life.

[1] Charles Elliott, *The Life of the Rev. Robert R. Roberts* (New York: G. Lane & C. B. Tippett, 1846), pp. 23 ff.

Finally the matter came to a head. One day a visitor from a distance came to the house. He chanced to ask one of the sisters, "Who is that rough looking hired man in the hunting shirt?" It was her brother! Both were embarrassed, as were the family when she told them later. Tom took it upon himself to remonstrate with his brother.

The effect was immediate and wholesome. Robert could not endure that they be ashamed of him. He determined to get better clothing, but would not ask his father for money. Instead he asked for leave from the farm when the fall work was done, and with a friend climbed Laurel Mountain to make tar. The young men made a shelter of chestnut bark and distilled pitch from the resinous sap of the pine trees. They cooked their food over a campfire, and lived in the open except for the warmth of the fire and the shelter of bark.

When they divided their earnings, Robert had money for new clothes. He bought a suit of yellow cashmere trousers and a green coat. He began to go out more with the young people. Little is said about his social habits; but in the bishop's narrative to Simpson there is a hint that one reason why he hesitated to join the church was a fear that, being young, he might bring discredit upon religion. There is always a reckless element among young men, and he must have known what they were doing, but there is not the slightest evidence that he shared in their excesses. He seemed to react instinctively against the obscenity and profanity so prevalent among men in frontier society.

When Robert was sixteen, an accident occurred which nearly cost his life. He was working in a sugarbush three miles north of the house, probably on the farm of Rogers, his sister Sarah's husband. He was cutting down a tree against which another tree had lodged. This was a dangerous thing to do, for he was obliged to chop under the leaning tree. He relied upon his agility to get out from under the trees when they began to fall. But he was not fast enough, and one of his legs was broken by a falling limb. He was brought home on the back of a horse by his brother-in-law. The boy recovered, but the leg was fractured again by a quick movement of his body when he turned to look at a stranger who was approaching the house on horseback. Later, his only comment on the accident was, "It gave me time to read."

Few books other than the Bible were accessible in the home at Ligonier. But the Bible is itself a library of the literature of a gifted people, and the King James Version, the only translation he knew, is exceptional English. He came to know much of the Bible by heart and was familiar with both the Old and New Testaments. This is shown by his later choice of sermon texts. One is surprised by unfamiliar passages from the less frequently read books.

Other books he read at the time were the writings of Wesley and Fletcher, loaned him by the itinerants when they thought he might become a preacher. Fortunately, Wesley and Fletcher were exceptional men and excellent writers. Of the two, Wesley had a scientific mind, an incisive style, and was a disciplined theologian. Roberts was loaned his *Sermons,* which Wesley had had printed for the instruction of his lay preachers. He also had access to Wesley's *Journal* which is one of the world's notable diaries.

John Fletcher, who greatly influenced Roberts' life, was a Swiss, educated at the University of Geneva. He came to England as a young military officer and became a tutor in an English family. Here he was converted under Wesley's preaching, and became Wesley's lifelong and ardent follower. Of all Wesley's converts he was the one most like the young collegians at Oxford, and the one whom Wesley desired to succeed him. The two volumes to which Roberts refers, *Checks to Antinomianism* and *An Appeal to Matter of Fact and Common Sense,* dealt with the conflict, intense at the time, between Calvinist theology and the teaching of Armenius. They involved the freedom of the will, the witness of the Spirit, holiness, and the deeper problems of philosophy. While Fletcher's writings were controversial, they were never personal or harsh. It is said of him: "He was one of the few controversialists who wrote without bitterness, through whose pages a spirit of love and deep devotion glows."

That Roberts, a boy of fourteen, could understand and be interested in these mature books reveals the quality of his mind. Writing of this period, he said:

> I had counsel, advice and prayers of the preachers, which I consider among the happiest circumstances of my early life as they took much pains with me. I began to read Fletcher's *Appeal,* Fletcher's *Checks,* and felt myself firmly established in the doctrines of the Methodists, and all that I desired to make me a Methodist was an evidence of my acceptance with God through the merits of the Redeemer,[2]

Doubtless, other books and stray periodicals from the East occasionally found their way to the Ligonier Valley and were eagerly read, but the Bible and the books mentioned were the boy's main reading during these impressionable years. In his personality and ministry Roberts was more like Fletcher than Wesley. Their environments and education were different, but they were much akin in outlook and devotion.

The winter of 1794-95, when Roberts and his young friend set up a turpentine camp on Laurel Mountain, marked a definite turning point in his life. He was coming to himself, and this seemingly unimportant experience was the first break. Ambition to have a life of his own—to adventure, to own land, to marry and have a home—was surging within him. He said little about what was going on in his mind until he acted, and what he did came as a surprise.

Sometime during the spring or summer of 1795 he made up

[2] Simpson ms., p. 5.

his mind that he must have more education. He may have read about colleges, but he knew they were not for him. What he wanted was to improve his writing and arithmetic. "In the eighteenth year of my age," he said, "I spent the winter in going to school some distance from my father's, so that I took boarding at a neighbor's. I made some proficiency in Writing and some in Arithmetic, and that is about all the schooling I received after coming to the western country." [3] A modest statement about an opportunity which meant so much to him.

The neighbor to whom he refers, a Mr. McCracken, lived three miles distant, and the school was in his cabin. Robert paid his board and room by beating out fibers of flax from the rotten stems of the plants. He went home on week ends to help his father flail wheat which had been stored in the barn.

The school was taught by a teacher from Ireland by the name of McAbee. Fortunately, he was a competent teacher. Realizing the seriousness of Roberts, he gave him special attention, and the two became friends. Years afterwards when Roberts, then Bishop Roberts, and his friend Elliott, were revisiting Ligonier, he met his former teacher. They sat on their horses and kept Elliott waiting two hours while they talked together.

[3] *Ibid.*, p. 6.

Chapter IV

Roberts' Conversion

A STRONGLY RELIGIOUS PEOPLE CAME INTO THE COUNTRY ABOUT Pittsburgh with the first settlers. A large immigration of Scotch Presbyterians, mostly from the north of Ireland, soon dominated the spiritual life of the area and have done so ever since. Into this wild country also came Asbury's zealous itinerants in 1783 and founded the famous Redstone circuit, centering at what is now Uniontown, fifty miles south of Ligonier. This was the first circuit west of the Allegheny Mountains. Bishop Roberts relates:

When I was about ten years of age, Methodists came to our neighborhood and preached about one-half mile from Father's house at Jacob Shane's. My brothers and sisters frequently heard them and very often amused themselves by making remarks upon the sermons and meetings. Father would not go to hear them as he believed them to be false prophets, and never did hear them until some of his family joined. His prejudices arose from the advice which his minister had given him concerning them.

After they had preached some time in the neighborhood, Mother went to hear them and took me with her. The preacher who preached that day I have never seen since. His name was James O'Call. He was not a regular traveling preacher, but sent to supply the place of the traveling preacher. His text was in the third chapter of the prophecy of Zephaniah, 8th verse. He was a "Son of Thunder." The sermon was an alarming one and produced much effect upon the congregation. It deeply affected my Mother. She wept much and it affected me. And had I not been under the influence of prejudice, as I believed my father knew their character and considered them false prophets, I should have been much more affected. Still with all my prejudice, the sermon seemed to be truth, and I knew that if it was true we must change our lives or be lost.

That day the first Methodist society was formed and several joined. My Mother would haave united with them had she not known the strong feelings of my Father. She probably knew something of experimental religion,[1] as her mother had heard Whitefield and was probably converted under his ministry. I remembered to have heard it said that Whitefield had set my grandmother crazy.

I think my mother did not return to meetings for some time owing to the objections of the family, and I did not go again for more than a year. But the young people still continued to attend and made remarks as formerly. Many things were said against class meetings and love feasts though they had not been in them.

Shortly after, a Quarterly Meeting was to be held twenty or thirty miles distant. As much was said about class meetings and love feasts, my sisters requested one of my brothers [John] to go with some young women who had joined the church, and after the love feast to bring back an account of what was done. Accordingly he went, although the young women knowing his carelessness and levity about religion, would rather at the time have been without his company. My sisters waited impatiently for his return as he did not return as soon as he expected. . . . To their great astonishment he had but little to say, appeared very solemn, and finally remarked that he believed they were very good people. This surprised me much as I had heard him frequently talking against them. My brothers and sisters continued to go to meetings but made fewer remarks. My father, mother, and I did not attend.

By this time the older children were grown. John was twenty-six, Sarah twenty-two, and the triplets eighteen. Robert was approaching adolescence. The religious situation in the famly was also changing.

By this time I began to be able to help my father on the farm. Returning home one evening I heard in a distant wood an unusual

[1] We would say *experiential,* but *experimental* was a common word at the time. It meant "could be demonstrated in personal experience."

noise. I knew not what it was, but at first supposed it to be a wild beast as there were then plenty in the country. I listened a while and finally went near and ascertained it was a human voice. I went toward it and there quite alone I found my sister Elizabeth engaged in prayer!

I listened to her supplications, and heard her pleading with God to have mercy upon her and to pardon her sins. I was somewhat alarmed, and wondered what crime she could have committed that she should be so deeply affected, as I thought nothing else could produce such deep agony of soul. After staying a while, I returned home without interrupting her, and kept the matter in my mind without informing anyone of the family.

He did not then know the effect of the preaching of these "Sons of Thunder," as he came to know later. Elizabeth's sensitive mind had been overwrought by the fear that she was a lost soul unless she experienced conversion. Shortly after, Sarah, Esther, and Elizabeth joined the society. Sarah had a vivid experience. Had she been a man, she would have been the first preacher in the family. She was ready at all times to pray in meetings when called upon and to bear witness to what God had done for her. The bishop said:

She affectionally told my father that he ought to keep family prayers. This he had frequently attended to on Sabbath but not regularly. The advice came with propriety from my sister, for owing to the failing health of my mother the care and management of the family came principally upon her.

He yielded to her advice and called the family together, took his Prayer Book and read prayers. But she was not satisfied, and told him she thought he ought to pray without his book. He then wrote a form of prayer and used that. Still she was not satisfied. He then said, "My child, pray yourself." She did so and kept up family worship for some time, some of the rest assisting. The children having joined, my mother also united with the society, and in a short time my brothers and my father also. Then I began to attend.[2]

[2] Simpson ms., p. 2 ff.

Finally this stubborn family, which had held aloof so long from the religious life of the neighborhood, broke through their prejudices and were again united in religion. The boy Robert, most spiritual and thoughtful of them all, was the last to surrender, not the father, as might have been expected. Soon the society was holding its meetings in the Roberts' cabin.

The gentle and heavily burdened mother needed what the little society gave her. She was sustained by the prayers and singing and by the friendship of the neighbor women who met in her home. She did not live long afterward and never saw the Shenango Valley. When she died or where her body lies is not known. She vanishes silently from the scene, and her valiant daughter Sarah took over the responsibility of the home.

The boy Robert had not yet come to his spiritual awakening, although it was near at hand. Let him tell it in his own words as he gave the story to Simpson in 1842:

One day about sunrise in the month of May, I was in a corner of the fence praying, when, I humbly trust, God for Christ's sake accepted me. Before that time I had frequently had sweet intimations of the goodness and mercy of the Lord. My heart was tender and I felt as if I could love God and his people. But yet, until that morning, my mind was not at rest. Then everything seemed changed. Nature wore a new aspect as I arose and went about my work with cheerfulness, though I own I did not then know whether I had received all that I should look for in conversion. I had never had such alarming views of my condition as some have experienced. My mind was gradually opened, and although I had always led a moral life I firmly believed that my heart must be changed. Owing to my youth I cannot now remember the precise day of my conversion, though the scene as it occurred that morning has ever been deeply printed in my memory. It happened in my fourteenth year, A.D., 1792.[3]

[3] *Ibid.*, p. 5.

This simple statement of a personal experience is worth study. Observe its reticence; he would understate rather than overstate; its intellectual honesty, shown by qualifying words and phrases. He had no overwhelming conviction of sin like his sister Elizabeth, which conviction was the orthodox pattern. His uncertainty had been as to his acceptance with God, which was what was meant at the time by the word *assurance* and by the phrase, *experimental religion.* His was not a dramatic experience, but a flooding of his being with love and peace and the age-old illumination of the natural word. The experience did not come to him at a mourner's bench, but as he was about to go to work in a sugarbush. The emotional quality was much like that of Wesley, except that Wesley was buffeted by doubts for a time afterward, while Roberts "arose and went about his work with cheerfulness." Roberts' awakening was in keeping with his irenic temper. He could never be dogmatic and was consequently especially helpful to people who could not enter the kingdom of heaven by violence.

The events which followed were not what might have been expected. He did not join the society until two years later, when he was sixteen. He was influenced by his father who thought him too young, but more by his own inhibitions which had been forming for so long. The preachers labored with him, but without avail. One preacher was severe, only to hurt him. Another with more insight gave him a class of children to instruct, which he accepted gladly and with which he was markedly successful.

This minister, a Mr. Bell, finally settled his membership in the society by a stratagem. Roberts was attending a class meeting, the leadership of which Bell assumed for the hour, but with the regular leader present. When he came to Robert, as was the custom, he turned to the leader and asked him if there would be any objection to placing Roberts' name on the roll? There being none, it was done. Roberts, taken by surprise, did not protest, but thought that "as the preacher had recorded his name, it should stay there."

These happenings naturally aroused speculation in the society about Robert's future. Might he become a preacher? They would have used the word *preacher,* instead of *minister* like the Presbyterians, or *pastor* like the Lutherans. Only the senior Roberts would have thought of *rector* or *priest.* Of course, the boy was too young for ordination, but the preachers became interested. They were always looking for promising candidates and took pride in these fruits of their ministry. They loaned or gave Robert religious books and talked with him from time to time as they came around the circuit on their travels.

The young Roberts was definitely interested, and there can be no doubt that his mind was fascinated by the idea of preaching. But the ministry was to him a sacred calling, so sacred that he drew back as unfitted, but so compelling that he could not give it up. This appears constantly in the bishop's narrative. Once, in a reminiscent mood, he told this story to his friend Elliott.

> One time when there was to be preaching in our home, I went out with Lewis, then thirteen, and preached so long that the meeting was closing when we got back. We tried to slip in but were observed. When Lewis was reproved by my father, he excused himself by saying, "Bob preached so long in the plum bushes that I could not get away." [4]

Under these circumstances one might think that Robert would have been an itinerant by the time he was twenty; but it took him six years to reach the decision. Like so many ministers, he was to go through travail of soul before he finally acted; but at the time he was too young to know what he wanted to do.

[4] *Ibid.*

Chapter V

Settlement of the Shenango Valley

When Roberts returned from his winter at school, his mind was in a ferment of newly awakened ambitions and desires. He wanted independence and freedom of action, and wanted them with all the intensity of his being. He reacted against the thought of the ministry, but could not get away from the feeling that it might be a call from God—a call which he could not disregard. But his great ambition was to own land and to have a home of his own.

The girl he wanted was one of the young women of the neighborhood whom he had known for a long time. But how could he tell her now? He was obligated to his father for three more years, and he had no money or prospect of earning, that he could see; so he came back to the farm at sugar-making time and kept his thoughts to himself.

The opportunity for independence came quickly and most unexpectedly. The Shenango Valley, a hundred miles to the north toward Lake Erie, had just been opened by the state of Pennsylvania for settlement. Settlers were offered four hundred acres of land at twenty dollars for each hundred acres, on condition that a cabin be built and twenty-five acres be brought under cultivation within five years. General Wayne had made peace with the Indians at Greenville the year before, and in 1796 the area was considered safe. The Indians were sullen, but their power was broken, and there was a garrison at the old French fort at the mouth of French Creek in the center of the area.

Roberts returned from school to find excitement in the neighborhood and four young men, including his brother Thomas, preparing to leave for the Shenango. He saw the opportunity and was at once in a fever of eagerness to join them. They thought him too young, but he was determined. They finally consented, on condition that he do the cooking and keep camp when they were exploring and hunting. How he won the consent of his father is not told. Probably Robert Morgan saw an opportunity for his boy to secure land. Out of his own holdings he had helped the older boys set up for themselves. But Robert seemed young to him, as indeed he was, and the father strictly charged Thomas to look after him.

The young men left Ligonier in early March. They went on foot, carrying food and blankets on their backs, and lived in the open. Four of them had rifles, Robert alone being without a gun. This is the first information that he had never hunted. They were caught by a snowstorm shortly after leaving the Ligonier Valley. They followed an old Indian trail over mountainous country. There were no roads, no bridges, no ferries. They forded swollen streams, or borrowed canoes, or built rafts of logs or felled trees across. Crossing the Allegheny at what is now Freeport, they explored the country nearby, but finding it unsuitable for farming, they continued farther north.

They had depended on their rifles for meat, but as yet no game had been seen, so the four older men set out on an all-day hunt, leaving Robert in camp. They were back in the afternoon without success, having seen no game or sign of game. An hour or two of daylight remaining, Robert asked his brother for the loan of his rifle, and Thomas reluctantly consented.

Robert had gone but a short distance when he saw two deer within easy range. In his excitement he had buck fever. He explained:

When I raised my rifle to shoot, my eyes suddenly watered and my hands shook so violently that I could not sight the gun. I leaned against a sapling, but the deer had seen me, and by the time I had recovered control they had disappeared into the thick woods.

Greatly chagrined, I pulled myself together and proceeded along the ridge. Once again my luck was with me. Looking down a hollow towards the creek I saw a mother bear with two cubs. I was on the windward and the bear did not sense my presence. Determined this time not to lose control I prepared to shoot from the knees. When the bear came within range it suddenly stood up and began to sniff the air. I fired at once. The bear fell and rolled on the ground, growling savagely. It stood up, fell again, and then recovering from shock made off with the cubs into the woods.

If I had reloaded the rifle and followed the wounded animal quickly, I should probably have got it; but I hurried back to camp and told what had happened. Hubank had not yet returned, and the three others, myself guiding, went in search of the bear expecting to find it dead or bady wounded; but without success. This was my first experience with big game. The men rallied me that night about the campfire, but they seemed to have a new respect for my luck in finding game.[1]

Two of the men, including his brother, did not like the country and decided to return home. Thomas did his best to persuade Robert to return with them. He had been charged by his father with his safety, but Robert would not consent. He was determined to carry out his purpose. Finally, Thomas left so little money that he thought his brother would soon be compelled to return home. Two of the other men, Caughey and Hubanks, decided to continue the journey with Roberts.

The experiences of these three men furnishes such a picture of the methods used by settlers searching for suitable land, that I follow their movements and adventures in some detail.

They traveled north for three days without meeting game or human beings. Their provisions were reduced to a small quantity

[1] Simpson ms., p. 6 ff.

of flour. Roberts, who alone knew how to cook or was inventive in devising a way, mixed the flour with water in a hollow chopped in a log, flattened the dough with his axe, and cut it into strips. He wound these around green sticks and cooked them before the fire. The men ate with relish the crude bread without butter or salt.

On the third day they struck the Shenango Trail which led from Pittsburgh to the old French fort at the mouth of French Creek, and then on to Lake Erie. First deer, then the Indians, then the French had worn the trail deep and clear.

They stopped for supplies at Cassewago and explored the vicinity; but finding the good land taken, turned back to the mouth of Conneaut Creek and followed the Kuskuskia trail which led to the Beaver River. Cutting across to Sandy Creek, the men made camp within two miles of where they finally located land. Here they found an abandoned camp of Indians who had gone down the Shenango in canoes.

Hiding their packs near the camp next morning, the travelers moved on to the Little Shenango at the crossing of a trail where Old Salem Church now stands within a mile of the Roberts' farm. They liked the country, but were cautious and decided to explore more thoroughly before deciding. They took no food with them, expecting to return to camp by nightfall, but they wandered off the trail and had to camp for the night without their packs and provisions. One of them had shot a squirrel which Roberts proceeded to broil over the fire. They were all tired, and Caughey and Hubank fell asleep. Roberts watched the squirrel for a time, but he, too, drowsed off, and when he awoke, it was burned to a cinder; so they passed the night supperless.

Next morning they started for camp, Caughey leading the way. He was newly arrived from Ireland and was inexperienced in the woods. They traveled for hours, Roberts protesting from time to time that they were going in the wrong direction. Finally

Caughey realized that he was lost and asked Roberts to act as guide. All differed as to the direction in which the camp lay, but they followed Roberts and reached it late in the day. This experience gave Roberts their confidence and an ascendancy in their undertakings.

After supper they rested for the night and in the morning set out for the crossing of the Little Shenango, taking their packs with them. Here they made a more permanent camp and proceeded to locate claims. This was no easy task, since they had to agree among themselves and then to lay out the boundaries of their claims. They followed lines established by government surveyors shortly before and marked by posts and blazes. None of them got just what he wanted, but they were satisfied—especially Roberts, who saw his dreams coming true. His land began not far north from the crossing of the Little Shenango and extended over the hill beyond Big Run, where he later built a gristmill, and then to the west. It was unbroken forest, with only an Indian trail leading through woods along the eastern boundary.

The men selected sites for their cabins. As spring was coming on, they let building the cabins wait, remained in their camp shelter of chestnut bark, and began clearing ground for corn and potatoes. They tramped twenty miles to Cassewago to buy seed. They paid three dollars a bushel for potatoes and two for corn. This accomplished, they helped one another build cabins.

We have a description of Roberts' cabin,[2] and, the stone walls of the spring house he later built are still in place. The cabin was twelve feet square, built of small unhewed logs, and covered with a roof of chestnut bark held in place by poles. A fireplace made of sticks and clay was cut through one end and a low door was made on one side. The door was fashioned by hand from split planks and swung on wooded hinges. The only light came from the fire, or through the open door, or through a small window to the

[2] Elliott, *op. cit.*, p. 77.

right of the fireplace. They were too busy to build floors and were content to sleep on balsam boughs.

The provisions of the three men were exhausted before their first harvests matured, a situation especially serious for Roberts, since the little money left him by his brother as well as his own was soon gone, and he could get no employment. He had no gun for hunting and was too sensitive to ask the loan of one. Caughey, learning of his plight, gave him money, and the three of them walked to Cassewago and brought back provisions on their backs.

Roberts was often depressed during the summer. He was young—but eighteen—homesick, and missed the social and religious life at Ligonier. Religion was like daily bread to him.

During that spring and summer [1796], my mind was often afflicted, and sometimes settled down in depression. Often I sat down upon the logs and wept and I found no relief but at a throne of grace. The causes of my depressions were four. First, I was away from home for the first time for any space longer than a week. Second, the circumstances of my absence as I had declined to return with my brother I feared might be disapproved of by my father, and for him I always felt a high regard. Third, I was every day getting more deeply in debt, and I never before had owed anything. Fourth, my principal cause was the absence of all religious services. Never before since experiencing religion had I been deprived of religious meetings. My classmate became careless in some measure and lost his relish for religious conversation. I knew nothing of the religious views of Caughey. The young men with whom we were associated for a while were very irreligious and among us we had but one Bible. Under the circumstances, though I believe I remained steadfast in religious integrity, yet often I was depressed, and many evenings did I weep before God until my heart was comforted. Shortly however before I left that place, returning from silent prayer, I heard a voice, and on listening I heard Caughey at prayer. This encouraged me much as I had not known him to be religious. But now I was able to converse with him on religious matters.[3]

[3] Simpson ms., p. 7 ff.

Their first crop of corn was destroyed by ground squirrels as fast as it germinated, but the potatoes did well. Having made the first required clearings and built the cabins, Roberts and Caughey decided to return to Ligonier to help with harvests, leaving Hubank to keep possession and gather the potatoes.

With knapsacks on their backs, the young men walked to the mouth of French Creek. Here they had a chance for jobs on a keelboat which was carrying supplies from Pittsburgh to Cassewago. Keelboats were long narrow vessels, speedier than flatboats, and were poled upstream. They could navigate small rivers at high water and had considerable carrying capacity. This particular boat had a crew of six men and was owned by a profane and drunken captain.

The rapids at the mouth of French Creek, where they met the boat, were difficult to ascend because of the swift current. The captain cursed and bullied his men, which Roberts and Caughey would not stand. They jumped off the boat and refused to go on. The captain relented and they continued the voyage to Cassewago. Here they helped unload the cargo, and finding the boat was to return immediately, continued as deck hands to Pittsburgh. Roberts was able to repay Caughey and to return home with a little money in his pocket.

The fifty-mile walk from Pittsburgh to Ligonier was quickly made under the joy of home-coming. They had been gone five months, but it seemed much longer. Roberts was bearded, his hair long, his clothes worn, his body lean but strong. He needed badly the cleanup which he got. The family had worried about him and had censured his brother for not bringing him back. They had not heard from him during these long months. At first, his father refused to let him return to the Shenango. Robert bided his time and went to work in the fields.

He was happy to be at home after the privations and isolation of the Shenango; home to good and abundant food, to his own people, and to his old friends and associations. He sought out the young woman he loved. He was welcomed at the next meeting of the little Methodist society of which he was a member. The family was proud and happy, Robert Morgan saying little, the older boys showing respect, the girls unrestrained in their affection. If only his mother could have welcomed him!

When the preacher spoke to him privately about a call to the ministry, the old worry came back to plague him again. He had almost forgotten it in the Shenango. He was perplexed and uncertain. He felt himself unfitted and unworthy to enter the sacred calling. He had never attempted to speak in public and could not be induced to do so. But deeper down was a harder struggle: how could he bring himself to abandon the project on which he had set his heart? The wandering life of an itinerant, the meager stipend, and the fact that married men were not admitted to any of the conferences, appalled him.

Roberts remained at the Ligonier during the fall until the harvests were gathered. He finally received the consent of his father to return to the Shenango. He was not yet of age and could not and would not go without it. Meanwhile neighbors had become interested and wanted to go along to take up land. His brother Thomas had changed his mind and was going back. Lewis, seventeen, was clamoring to join them; but Lewis was needed on the farm now that Robert was leaving, and their father consented only on condition that he return for the spring work. At last in early March a company of nine men, with heavily laden pack horses, left for the Shenango. Roberts was their leader. Without intention, and unaware of what he was doing, Roberts was becoming an organizer of migration into the Ohio River Basin. Twenty years later he was to do the same in southern Indiana.

Thomas was now pleased with the Shenango country and selected a claim; but having done so, he left Stephen Riley with his brother to make the improvements required, and returned to his farm at Ligonier. This time, however, he left money, tools, and provisions. Roberts brought with him a new and excellent rifle. How he came by it is not told. Probably his father, knowing the need and impressed by the stories of his skill with game, had given him one. These Pennsylvania rifles were handmade and greatly coveted by hunters. They gave them colorful names after their women, as men on the seaboard named their boats. They were heavy guns and had long slender rifled barrels, flint locks, and stalks of polished walnut.

A month after their arrival Roberts and Stephen Riley left on a Sunday morning to buy maple sugar at an Indian camp on Sandy Creek. They went on Sunday, against their custom, because they did not know the way and could go with an Indian who was making the trip. As always they carried rifles. One of them missed a shot at a distant deer. They bought all the sugar they could get for three dollars and started home. Darkness caught them in a big swamp from which they could not find their way that night. Rain set in and put out their campfire. A hungry panther began to scream nearby and prowled around them throughout the night. A fire would have frightened the big cat, but they could not kindle the wet wood, so they had to stand guard through a miserable night. Unhappily, also the sugar melted in the rain. Roberts thought this misfortune a judgment upon them for breaking the Sabbath, and would never after carry a rifle on Sunday.

Returning to their clearings, the men worked steadily through the spring months without incident and consumed provisions freely, expecting the return of Thomas with supplies; but his coming was delayed. Food and money became exhausted. Riley hired himself out to another man, but Roberts kept at work. Game was scarce. Probably the does were secluded with their fawns, and the bucks had gone into the mountains. Roberts was reduced for a month to a diet of squirrels. When he could endure it no longer, he started for the fort at French Creek to pawn his rifle for food. Squirrels were considered a dainty meat, but he could never afterward be induced to eat them.

Six miles out toward the fort, hungry and dejected, he met his father, his brother, Thomas, Lewis, and his sister Elizabeth! With them were four horses loaded with supplies, and four cows which they had driven from Ligonier. Evidently, they had come to stay. Elizabeth jumped from her horse, burst into tears, and embraced her brother. Roberts said afterward that he felt "like Jacob when he saw the wagons which Joseph had sent for him." [4]

[4] Elliott, *op. cit.*, p. 50.

Chapter VI

Roberts' Sister Elizabeth

ROBERTS' FATHER AND TWO BROTHERS REMAINED UNTIL NOVEMBER. Before they left they assisted in building a shelter for the stock they had driven from Ligioner and helped accumulate fodder for the winter. They then returned to Ligonier, but left much needed supplies and equipment. Elizabeth, to his great joy, decided to remain with her brother over the winter. They were both young—he only eighteen; she, twenty-five.

With the coming of this favorite sister, life in the drab little cabin took on color and cheerfulness. It became a home instead of a shelter from rain and winter cold. It was small for the needs of a home, only twelve by twelve. They had to stoop to enter the door; and once the door was closed, the interior was dark except for candlelight or the flames from the fire. She transformed the place by her woman's skill and the magic of her presence. She was the first white woman in the valley. The lonely men of the wilderness, separated from their womenfolk, were hungry for the sight of her.

The Shenango Valley was by this time beginning to attract settlers. The Roberts' cabin lay alongside the main trail leading to the North, and many came to the door seeking information and sometimes shelter. Most were poor, often hungry, their clothing badly worn by the rough life of the forest. Thomas Jolly, one of the settlers, lived three months on bad potatoes. His teeth loosened, and he became a shadow of his former self. When the cabin of Caughey burned about this time, five neighbors helped him rebuild it in a day, but they worked without food.

The plight of many of these men awakened the compassion of Elizabeth. She and her brother had food in their cabin—milk and butter, and an abundance of venison—and, like all the Roberts girls, she was an excellent cook. She soon became the good angel of the valley. Strangers were given shelter for the night. This was nothing new on the frontier, except for the friendliness of their welcome and the cleanliness of the place. People heard about her—such news spreads quickly—and found excuses to come their way. She served food without being asked, reading their faces. She would invite men, passing along the trail, who looked hungry to come in for food. When she heard of a sick neighbor, she sent by her brother such remedies as they had. She cut up ticking she had woven at Ligonier and brought with her for their own beds, and made shirts for men whose clothing was in shreds. Such garments could not be bought nearer than Cassewago, twenty miles distant; and few had the money to buy.

Elizabeth seemed to awaken and to come to full expression of her natural gifts, for which she needed only opportunity and responsibility. She revealed family traits—sympathy, unselfishness, emotional depth—which were marked also in her brother.

On the ninth of November a heavy snow began to fall and continued for three days. It sifted down a foot deep in the woods around them. Deer herded together at night for safety against hungry wolves. As soon as the storm abated and deer could be tracked in the snow, Roberts took his rifle and went into the woods.

Writing of this opening of his first and to him memorable winter's hunting, Roberts said:

I laid up a good stock of provisions and plenty of salt, had, besides my own rifle, several others left in my care, and a plentiful supply of ammunition. I designed spending the winter in hunting. Chestnuts were plenty and I had collected a quantity of them. I had also found a bee tree and had plenty of honey. On the ninth of November, 1797, it began to snow and continued for two days and nights. When it ceased it was about 12 to 15 inches deep. I commenced hunting, and continued for three days. It sifted down a foot deep in the woods to provide wood, and fodder my cattle. Upwards of two weeks I hunted thus every day and killed nothing, always overshooting the deer. I came home at night much fatigued. My sister pleaded with me to desist lest I should perish and she too. Still I had an unconquerable desire to be a hunter.

One morning I arose and some fresh snow had fallen. I went toward the creek, came across a large flock of wild turkeys which with difficulty could get through the snow. Thinking I could call them I took a circuit to get around them. Then ahead of them I saw a large chestnut tree hollow and a hole burnt through. I stepped in and put my gun through to fire as they came up. In a few minutes a buck of the largest class came walking along only a few rods from the tree. I had heard hunters say that if a person called a deer would stop. I made some noise and he stopped and raised his head. I fired immediately. I stepped out to see my deer and I saw him running back as fast as he could run. I felt despondent. I thought I never could have a better chance and I might as well give up. But, loading the rifle I went to his tracks, saw some blood and followed them and soon found him dead. I was so rejoiced I left him and told my sister what I had done. I went back and skinned him, took meat home on my shoulder and felt satisfied. Next morning early I saw another deer and pursued him. As he turned on his track, I shot, and watched him until he fell. Then I continued hunting successfully.[1]

Another day he shot a large buck, and, thinking it dead, went up uncautiously to examine it. The animal was not seriously wounded, and seeing him approach, sprang up and attacked him furiously with antlers and sharp front hoofs. When the buck attempted to gore him, Roberts grasped his antlers. The buck reared and plunged, lifted Roberts from his feet again and again, and tore his clothing and flesh with antlers and hoofs. They fell

[1] Simpson ms., pp. 19 ff.

and rolled together down a hill, Roberts holding desperately to the animal's horns, until they came under a fallen tree which lay across and above the trail. Here the buck could not get to his feet, and Roberts was able to kill the animal with his hunting knife.[2] Roberts was laid up two weeks from this encounter, but he began hunting again as soon as he had recovered.

The effect upon Elizabeth was more serious than upon her brother. When he did not return from a hunt before dark, and the night wore on, she became frantic. She was not only alarmed for her brother, but she was alone in a wild country. She would climb to the roof and call into the night. Since Roberts knew her anxiety, one might ask, why did he not return earlier? Why did he not make it a point never to be out overnight?

One answer a hunter will understand. When a hunter follows the tracks of a deer, especially a wounded animal, he keeps right on. Every impulse of the age-old instinct pulls him forward until he comes up with the quarry. A fundamental trait of Roberts, his persistence, also kept him going. He was determined to become a good hunter and it was his way, once started, to persist. Hunting was also the one way at Shenango to get ready money. A deer pelt brought twenty-five cents a pound at Greenville and more at Pittsburgh, and they were greatly in need of money.

By the end of that winter Roberts had become a skilled hunter. He knew the country in all directions and had learned the habits and feeding grounds of the deer. He had also become an expert with the rifle—no more buck fever, no failing to reload immediately, no overshooting the deer. Like the fabled Nimrod of Genesis, he had become "a mighty hunter before the Lord." He had not expected to hunt for fur-bearing animals, but finding it profitable, studied the habits of the racoon, fox, mink, and otter. He became learned in the lore of the forest and fascinated by its

[2] Elliott, *op. cit.*, pp. 54-55.

solitudes. The love of the wild became a passion that remained with him the rest of his life.

Late one night that spring the dog, sleeping by the fireplace, awakened suddenly and began barking furiously. Elizabeth arose and looking out, saw the shadowy form of a man approaching in the darkness. Roberts cautioned his sister to get back from the door and took down his rifle. The fear of Indians was never absent from the settlers, so recent were the massacres. The man proved to be his friend Caughey bringing with him Roberts' sister Esther as a bride. Their father and their brothers, John and Lewis, were not far behind and arrived a half-hour later. There was little sleep in the cabin the rest of the night. They learned that their father had sold a part of his land at Ligonier, and that the family, except John, were coming permanently to the Little Shenango. John never left Ligonier.

Within two years Roberts' ambitions were being realized beyond his hopes. At twenty he had become the leader of the family. They had sought to restrain him from the Shenango adventure two years before, thinking him too young, but now they were following his lead into the new country. Many of them were to follow him later into Indiana.

In April Robert and Lewis went to Ligonier to bring their sisters Nancy and Sophia and their maternal grandfather, Thomas Richford, who was nearing ninety-three, to Shenango. John returned with them to Ligonier. His sister Sarah had married at Ligonier and remained at the old home.

Elliott writes:

> During the whole journey they lay out every night. Nancy Roberts drove three cows and two pet pigs, carrying an axe on her shoulder, and walking all the way. Sarah walked also and carried a spinning wheel on her shoulder, beside taking care of her grand-father much of the journey. Sophia sometimes rode behind the pack on one of

the horses, and sometimes walked. The old man, though very feeble and somewhat peevish, received no injury by the journey.[3]

In November the hunting season opened again. Robert, his brother Lewis, and John McGranahan, who later married Nancy and became a noted hunter, joined in hunting. When the season ended, they packed sixty deerskins and pelts of raccoons and other fur-bearing animals to market.

Transportation was the most difficult problem during the pioneer era. At a distance from the big streams everything had to be carried on men's backs or on pack animals. It was impossible to market farm produce except among neighbors, and mostly by barter. Roberts' experience with a flatboat led him, on one of his trips to Ligonier, to buy a pirogue at Connelsville and to attempt to carry back a load of supplies by water. A pirogue is a large canoe hollowed out of a big tree. Three men took the well-loaded pirogue down the Youghiogheny and Ohio, and up the Beaver, Shenango, and Little Shenango rivers to the crossing at Salem Church, a mile and a half from the Roberts' place. One of the men was William Lindsey who later married Elizabeth.

They succeeded, but it was a hazardous voyage and was not repeated. They came near disaster at the falls of the Beaver. At the mouth of the Shenango, which was flooded, their poles could not reach bottom, and they were obliged to leave the pirogue with one of the men. Thinking they were near the settlement and could reach it by night, they started overland for Shenango.

Roberts said:

We traveled all day and were obliged to camp at night without provisions. A snow storm came on before morning, and we found ourselves in the wilderness where every path was so obscured that we could not ascertain our course with any certainty. In the evening we found a moccasin track which we supposed to have been made

[3] *Ibid.*, p. 65.

by an Indian. We followed it, and it led us to some Indian camps on the banks of the Shenango. The leading Indian, Captain Petty, could speak English and from him we learned we were only six or eight miles up the river from the place we had left our canoes on Saturday morning. We had traveled two days to but little purpose.

We were all of course very hungry, having fasted two days and a night and performing the hard labor of traveling in the snow. Captain Petty promised to provide some victuals for us. After the use of a camp had been given us, we waited with no small degree of impatience for the promised supplies as what we had gone through was not well calculated to preserve, much less improve the temper. The time of waiting seemed very long to us, and finally I went to Captain Petty and told him we were exceedingly hungry. He replied, "The women are cooking."

Shortly two squaws came along with a little brass kettle, holding one and a half or two gallons, and full of venison which had been cut in pieces not too large to be taken into the mouth at once, and boiled in bears' oil. No salt was furnished but we had some with us which of course we used. Mr. Gurwell, being the oldest, was brought a little hominy but the rest had none. Shortly a hunter came in with a deer, a quarter of which was sent to the strangers as their share. . . .

I went home and found my sister making sugar. She had made a quantity and was worn down with fatigue. She had on hand a great deal of sugar water and partly made syrup. I agreed to relieve her that night and let her rest at the house. I felt sorry, and thought I could fill up the kettles and then lie down to rest. Sometime, perhaps about midnight, I filled the kettles, laid down and fell asleep. The kettle of the strongest syrup boiled over into the fire. The noise awakened me and it seemed as if the flame was five or six feet high. I jumped up in fright, caught up some water in a pail and threw it into the kettle; with the result that the kettle was split and all the syrup went into the fire. This finished my syrup making for the night.[4]

Hunting now gave place to the more prosaic work of the farm. Deer, unmolested by hunters, were bearing their young and need only fear the less dangerous wolves and panthers. Life went on quietly at the Roberts' cabin until midsummer, when his

[4] Simpson ms., pp. 20, 21.

life was again disrupted by Elizabeth's marriage to William Lindsey on August 17. Lindsey was one of the young men who had come with Roberts the second year. His claim of 410 acres adjoined Roberts' land on the north.

With her marriage Elizabeth becomes a distant figure in the dim past. This much is known: she became the mother of eight children during the next fifteen years and died prematurely at forty-two. "At her death," says Virgil Johnson, "her children were scattered over the neighborhood." Roberts took Esther, her first-born, with him to Indiana and reared her as his own. Lindsey remarried soon and became the father of another family of eight children. Her body lies in the Stephenson burying ground a mile south from her home and in sight of Old Salem Church.

I stood by Elizabeth's grave with emotion in the summer of 1951, thinking of the winter of 1797-98 when she was the only woman in the valley and its good angel, and of her hardships and premature death. May God bless her valiant spirit.

Chapter VII

Marriage

ROBERTS RETURNED TO A LONELY CABIN AFTER HIS SISTER'S marriage. Previous to her coming his mind was on his work, and he had little concern about where he lived, except as a shelter from rain and cold and a place to sleep. His sister had transformed the cabin by her woman's presence. Now that she had gone, the stark reality of the low door, the dark interior, and the cramped quarters, oppressed him. He determined to hasten his own marriage. Once he had made up his mind, he acted with his usual resolution.

Marriage had seemed remote to him since he was still under age and had so little to offer a woman. But now he would wait no longer, except that he could not leave Shenango until after the fall harvests and the winter's hunting. The pelts and furs of the hunt were his one source for the money he needed.

The hunting season of 1798-99 was unusually successful. In late January Robert and his brother Lewis packed three horses with pelts and walked beside them from the Little Shenango to Greensburg, where the pelts were sold to advantage. Then he was free. The two men hurried on to their home at Ligonier and to the glamorous associations of their young friends. Two weeks later, in mid-January of 1799, Elizabeth Oldham and Robert Richford Roberts were married.

This is all that is known about the wedding. Nobody kept an account of it, or if one of the family wrote to a friend, the letter has disappeared. Roberts makes no mention of the marriage in the manuscript of 1842. He may have thought it a private matter in which the church would not be interested. Elliott got the information about the wedding journey from Elizabeth in the summer of 1843, after her husband's death; but he missed an unusual story of married love and devotion which continued through a lifetime. The story is told in fragments of letters, the originals of which have been lost; in chance references in books of the period, but mainly in the way they lived and worked together.

It is known that she came from York, Pennsylvania, and that the two families had been friends in Maryland. The Robertses may have been responsible for the Oldham family's coming to the Ligonier Valley. The young people knew each other, but beyond this is conjecture. That she was deeply religious, that she was capable, that she had been carefully taught the arts of homemaking and the household industries of the time, presumably by an equally capable mother, became evident when they reached Shenango and she took charge of the home.

Their honeymoon was the return journey to Shenango on horseback through the mountains of western Pennsylvania, when that part of the state was still a wilderness. There were no roads for wagons, no bridges or ferries over streams, no inns; and the ground was covered with snow. The trail led over shoulders of the Alleghenies and through thickets, deep woods, and narrow valleys. It would seem a formidable journey to young people of the present time; but to them it was not unusual, and as romantic a honeymoon as one today by airplane or automobile.

They left in February to get to Shenango in time for sugar making. To miss the flow of sap in the hard maples when the spring thaws set in would have meant to be without sugar the rest of the year. The brothers packed the three horses with household goods, provisions, and tools for work, and included three bulky iron kettles for boiling down the maple sap. Two of the kettles were broken against rocks on the journey. They planned that Elizabeth should ride one of the horses, but she preferred to walk with them most of the way rather than to ride along the narrow trails.

Late in the afternoon of the third day out night fell, and Roberts lost the trail in the darkness. His brother had gone ahead with two of the horses carrying the provisions. They were passing through underbrush along a stream at the time, and Roberts did not think it safe to hunt for the trail in the darkness. He decided to make camp where they were. The ground was deep in snow and they had no food, but there were blankets in the packs on Elizabeth's horse.

Roberts had spent many nights in the open in worse weather and knew what to do. With his axe he cleared a space near a fallen pine tree from which he could chop dry wood, and soon he had a fire blazing. Then he removed the packs from the horse and allowed the animal to browse on the buds of the bushes around. They were nourishing food to the hungry creature. After taking care of the horse, he made a thick bed of boughs, laying the stems underneath. Over this he spread their blankets. Stripping bark from a chestnut tree, he laid a sloping roof, open toward the fire, over the bed of boughs. All they lacked was food. The air was crisp, but the fire was warm and cheerful. They sat on the blankets under the lean-to, watching the flames, glad to be alone together; and as they talked, they forgot their hunger.

Suddenly they were startled by the deep-throated baying of timber wolves, first at a distance but coming rapidly nearer, howling as they ran. The frightened horse came to the fire for safety, and Elizabeth drew close to her husband in fear. "They will surely eat us before morning," she said in alarm.

"No, Betsey, they will not eat us," he assured her. "They are afraid of fire. If I throw a brand at them, they will scatter. I will keep the fire burning through the night. You can lie down when you feel like it and go to sleep in safety."

She could see the shadowy forms of the wolves, the firelight shining in their eyes in the darkness. They had ceased baying and were gazing intently at the fire. Robert threw a brand at them. They scattered, as he had said, and finally left the vicinity of the camp. Elizabeth grew drowsy in the warmth of the fire, and, wrapping her blanket about her, fell asleep.

Roberts found the trail next morning without difficulty, and they caught up with Lewis in the course of an hour. He had spent the night at a hunter's cabin. The man had killed a bear the day before, and the place was covered with grease from the rendering of the fat. When Elizabeth looked in, she drew back and whispered to her husband, "I am glad we lost our way last night. Let us go on." Hungry though they were, they declined the kindly offer of food, and proceeding on their way, ate breakfast beside the trail in the clean forest.

They were five days on the journey from Ligonier to the Shenango Valley—days of exposure and hard travel, but also of singular happiness, for they were beginning life together. Like all young people they saw the future in glowing colors, and the privations of the journey seemed of little consequence.

When Robert finally led Elizabeth up the path to his cabin door, his heart misgave him. "It is such a little place," he said. "I am ashamed to bring you here, but I will build you a better one soon."

"Don't worry about the cabin," she answered. "It is our home. You built it with your own hands when you came to this country two years ago. We will work together. I am not afraid of work."

They stooped and entered the dim interior. Slowly, as their eyes adjusted to the semidarkness, table, fireplace, a bench, and the rough frame of a bed against the wall, began to appear. The two stood in silence, until he could stand the oppression no longer.

"I will build a fire," he exclaimed. "The room is cold and we need light."

She waited while he brought in wood and watched him kindle a fire with flint and tinder. Soon it was blazing, and the bare room was glorified with light. Then she began to put the room in order. He carried water from the nearby spring and swung a kettle above the flames. He unstrapped the packs from the horses' backs and laid the bundles in a corner of the room, untying them for her convenience. Then, while she worked, he went out to care for the animals and to prepare a shelter for them against the cold night.

When he returned, the place was clean as if a miracle had been wrought. Fresh sheets and blankets, with pillows and a coverlet, lay over the bed. A white linen cloth covered the table, and their few new dishes were laid for supper. He watched her place potatoes in hot ashes and cover them with coals, mix corn meal in a skillet, and cut slices of ham for another skillet. When they sat down to the table and bowed their heads for the blessing, the fervor of his prayer revealed his gratitude.

They were barely settled when the spring thaw came and sugar making began. The camp lay a mile to the south, along the Little Shenango. Robert and Lewis had hewed small troughs from poplar trees to catch the sap from the maples, and a huge trough had been set up on a rise of ground near the stream for collecting the sap.

Maple sugar was an important commodity to the people of the frontier, as it had been ot the Indians before them. Commercial sugar was expensive on the frontier and hard to get. Maple sugar was to be had for the making. It was their sweetening for cooking, their candy, and their syrup for corn bread and pancakes. To us it is a luxury; to them, a necessity. Indians in the north country made it from time immemorial.

The scene was interesting and animated. All worked—Robert, Elizabeth, his sister Nancy (now a young woman), and a young nephew John. They carried the sweet sap from overflowing troughs, kept the fires burning, stirred the kettles with watchful eyes, and sugared off at the right time. The output of the day was carried to the cabin for storage when they came home at night.

One day they worked far into the night to sugar off. This had to be done once the fires had been started. There was a heavy storm upstream which did not reach them, but they could hear the thunder. Roberts noticed that the stream was rising, but he had no misgivings. Darkness came, but they kept on working, unaware of the danger. Suddenly Roberts realized that the stream was bank high and discovered that an old channel behind them was a seething flood, cutting them off from higher ground.

There was nothing to do but wait for morning. The water kept rising and threatened the ground where the fires were burning. Soon they were forced to take refuge on the trunk of a large tree which had fallen alongside the stream. Roberts emptied the big trough, put earth in the bottom, and made a fire to keep them warm. But the fire burned through, and they were forced to walk up and down the fallen tree to keep from freezing while the water swirled beneath. The situation was frightening in the extreme.

The night passed slowly—seemingly endless—but courage and resourcefulness carried them through. When day began to break and there was light enough to see, Roberts undertook to extricate them. He waded the shallower water, probing in advance with a pole, but coming to the channel, found it beyond his depth. Returning for the axe, he felled a tree over which he passed in safety. Coming back, he took them one at a time to the dry land, wading beside them in the shallows and steadying them over the tree. Wet and cold but grateful to be out of danger, they hurried home to the warmth of a fire and to food. Strangely, none of them became ill from the exposure, but sugar making was ended for the season.[1]

As spring ploughing was still six weeks off, Robert and Lewis cleared a field for flax and made improvements about the cabin. Elizabeth wanted flax for linen, which she knew how to weave. Late in summer, in the interval before harvest, Robert built her a loom. He seemed to be able to make anything needed on the farm.

When frost left the ground, spring work began. He now had horses for plowing and fields for planting. Robert did the rough work, but Elizabeth helped in planting time. She was to do such work in after years when her husband was absent on episcopal journeys and she was left to direct the farm. She also took over much of the care of the garden. They worked together happily through the spring and summer and the months of harvest. When the first snows fell in November, he resumed hunting. So passed the next three years.

By 1799 the valley was filling with settlers—most of them from the Roberts clan, their connections by marriage and friends from the Ligonier Valley. Women were now in cabins, and children began to appear in the doorways. There was visiting back and forth, and life was no longer solitary. Neighbor helped neighbor in sickness and misfortune, and women their sisters in childbirth. Community life was on the simplest cultural level. There was not a college man, or a suit of clothes from London, or a house more spacious than a single-room log cabin in the valley.

Religion also had entered the Shenango with the earliest settlers. Roberts, Caughey, and Hubanks, who were the first to take up land, were members of the Methodist society in Ligonier. After the Robertses, who were Welsh, most settlers came from Ireland and were either Presbyterians or converts of Wesley during his missions in Ireland. Two years after the winter of 1796-97 the first Methodist society was organized. By then most of the

[1] Elliott, *op. cit.*, pp. 84-86.

Roberts family and neighbors from the Ligonier society had come to the Shenango, and were numerous enough to form a class and hold prayer meetings in their cabins.

The organization of the first class was due to the zeal of Jacob Gurwell, a local preacher. He had come from Ligonier with Roberts on the canoe voyage from Connelsville and had entered land. He was a humble but good man, a farmer like the rest of them, but had a gift of speech and a fire burning in his soul. No sooner had he built his cabin than he began holding meetings on Sundays.

Local preachers like Gurwell were a primary influence in the spread of the Methodist societies. They kept the church abreast of the movement of population during the great migration. They were selected for their gifts and character by the itinerants from laymen, and were given training for their duties. Only men who had a spiritual experience and had shown a zeal for souls were commissioned. They received no compensation, unless, as occasionally happened, they were asked to give their whole time to a circuit. In the books of the time they are given the title "Reverend." For example, John Rankin of Mississippi, who built a great house on the Pearl River and had a hundred slaves on his plantation, was known as "Rev. John Rankin," although he was never a member of the Mississippi Conference. Elliott calls Gurwell "Rev. Jacob Gurwell."

Two years later Thomas McClelland came from Ireland and took up land in the valley. He had been a traveling preacher under Wesley for a time and was then a local preacher. He also had some education and a flair for writing. He and Roberts became friends and began writing and exchanging verse and prose. What they wrote was not important except for its influence upon Roberts' intellectual development. It quickened his mind and stimulated his natural gift of expression.

Roberts was chosen class leader of the society at its beginning.

He protested, but Gurwell and the society persisted. When he finally accepted, he could not be induced to question the members of the class and to give them counsel, as was the custom. His father, his brothers, sisters, and neighbors were members, some of them older than he. How could he question and advise them? Gurwell labored with him, but without avail. Roberts suggested that Caughey take his place, but Caughey talked too much, and Roberts was recalled.

So began Old Salem Church, the first Methodist church in the Erie Conference. It became in time a preaching appointment on the Shenango circuit and had monthly visits from the preachers in charge. Among them was Asa Shinn, a gifted young man who afterward became a leader of the Methodist Protestant Church. The congregation met first in Gurwell's cabin, then in Roberts', finally in a log church built at the crossing of the Little Shenango a mile south of Roberts' cabin. This was followed by a frame building which Bishop Roberts dedicated. It burned and the present structure was erected on the foundations.

Although but slightly over twenty-one, Roberts had become the leader of the community. The situation was unusual in that there was no organization in the valley except the little Methodist class, and no formal expressions of leadership. He would have been the last to recognize that he had such influence, but he did say to Simpson that his cabin had become the center of the community. Leadership had come to him naturally because he had the initiative and resourcefulness that inspire confidence.

Two of the older members of the Roberts family died shortly after Roberts' marriage. The first to go was Thomas Richford, his mother's father, who died on September 8, 1800. He was over ninety years of age. Robert Morgan Roberts followed a year later on February 28, 1801.

Chapter VIII

They Left All to Follow Christ

ELIZABETH HAD BEEN AT SHENANGO BUT A SHORT WHILE WHEN she became involved in Roberts' religious difficulties. They were to harass her for the next three years, and to plague him also until he finally yielded to what he felt to be the call of Christ.

He was so unsettled that he neglected his work, an unusual thing for him to do. His sister Nancy said to a friend after the bishop's death:

> Frequently, after digging up a few grubs or cutting down a tree or two, Robert would sit down and reflect on his situation the remainder of the day. He would sometimes leave his horses standing at the plow while he sat on the beam thinking; or he would go into the nearby woods to pray, or to preach to the trees.

Such experiences are not unusual to men who feel a call to the sacred vocation. Christ was driven into the wilderness when the consciousness of his mission came to him at the Jordan. Paul retired into Arabia and remained three years after his experience on the road to Damascus, so great was his agitation. He relates the experience in the Epistle to the Galatians.

Roberts' habit of "preaching to the trees" is interesting. He fought against the call to the ministry, but at the same time was fascinated by preaching. You will remember that when a boy he would preach to his brother Lewis and his younger sisters at times when other boys would be hunting rabbits. He would listen to the preachers and then go out and try for himself. He was doing this again at Shenango except that now he went into the woods alone. Without being aware of what he was doing, he was giving himself excellent training in speech. In speaking aloud, even to the trees, his logical mind corrected faults of construction and developed skill in the use of words.

He was also training his voice, which was deep and musical. He had an accurate ear for sounds, which was both natural and had been sharpened by hunting; for in the forest the hunter learns to see the slightest movement of an animal and hears the faintest sound. He had also the poet's sensitiveness to the music of words. When Richard Thompson, himself an effective speaker, heard him for the first time in the open air, he noted the quality of his voice, and the fact that he had it under control like a good actor.

But for all his speaking to the trees, he could not be induced to speak at the meetings of the little society. The preachers, sensing his vocation, were at their wits end to prevail upon him. Elizabeth told Elliott an incident about his reticence:

One morning Robert had gone into the woods with his gun and came back with four wild turkeys. There was to be a Christmas service at one of the neighbors on a weekday. When he got home, he said, "Come, Betsey, it's time to go to meeting." So they left the turkeys in the house and went to brother Gurwell's where the meeting was to be held. After the sermon the preacher, Brother McClelland, called upon Robert to conclude with an exhortation. He was so frightened and disconcerted that he immediately left the house and went to the barn.[1]

Pressure upon Roberts to enter the ministry, both from the preachers and from within himself, became persistent. He had gone so far as to accept the leadership of the class and to hold

[1] Elliott, *op. cit.*, p. 91.

neighborhood prayer meetings, but that was all. This is what he dictated to Simpson:

> I continued to hold prayer meetings as before. I went with the local preachers to their meetings and could generally conclude them by singing and prayer. The country was filling up with people and we had some large congregations. The local preacher McClelland was perhaps the first man who ever talked to me about the propriety of speaking in public. After conversing several times with me, he firmly believed it to be my duty to break through difficulties and commence preaching. He wrote a long letter, purporting to be a dream, and slipped it into my pocket. I pursued the same course until 1801, my mind still laboring under the same impressions which frequently made me uneasy.[2]

But there were other difficulties. He was deeply absorbed in the development of his land at Shenango. It was a consuming passion for which, without capital, he had given prodigious labor. To abandon this ambition for an uncertain profession which could offer no permanent home, no security, no independence, no satisfaction for his love of the soil, was to reverse the current of his life.

Then, too, Roberts was married, and happily married. He and Elizabeth were each well fitted for the life at Shenango. He would have become an important landowner and citizen, as he did a quarter of a century later at Lawrenceport. They might reasonably expect children, and from those they took into their home as their own we may be sure they wanted children.

They both knew that the conferences were averse to accepting married preachers. In fact, Roberts was the first married man to be admitted to a Methodist conference in America. The reason for the policy was the cost of maintenance, which included moving preachers, often long distances, every year, frequently every six months. A single preacher could mount his horse, load his saddle-

[2] Simpson ms., pp. 22-23.

bags, and be off on receipt of a letter from Asbury assigning him to another circuit.

No itinerant as yet received a salary, and there was no dependable income. The stewards of each society collected quarterage every three months from people who had little money, and gave it to the preacher. He never knew how much it would be and could be certain only that the amount would be small. He could be sure that he would be given food and shelter in friendly homes, and care for his horse. There were only two parsonages in all the widespread circuits—St. George's at Philadelphia and the Light Street house at Baltimore. Under such a system, which so completely sacrificed the preacher to his work, it was considered desirable that he should have no entanglements.

We do not know the reaction of Elizabeth during the early days of their marriage, but the prospect of the itinerancy could not have been inviting. She would have no settled home. He would be absent on the circuits of from twenty to forty appointments all but a few days every month. If she made a few friends, she would be separated from them within a year. The wretched stipend designed for single men could not maintain them. How could she possibly care for the children they ardently desired and hoped for? There must have been long and anxious discussions between them about these matters. His own family at Shenango is known to have been opposed to his becoming a preacher.

The situation was baffling in the extreme, and it is not surprising that he lost his capacity for effective work. His wife remarked forty years later that he seemed to succeed at nothing he undertook until the matter was settled. Nothing but a compelling conviction that it was the will of God could have induced him to become an itinerant preacher.

Then, too, they were young. He was not yet twenty-one when they married, and she but twenty-two. They were at the age of students in college, but with no such advantages. Life looked secure and promising to them where they were.

Their decision was reached one night as they sat before the fire, the flames lighting up their young faces. They talked long, in quiet voices, going over the problem that had shadowed their home for three baffling years. She was the one person to whom he could talk freely.

Finally, she said, "Robert, lay your head on my lap"—something he liked to do when he came home from a long day in the woods. She drew her fingers through his hair and pushed it back from his forehead. He lay in silence for a while, gazing at the fire.

Then she spoke again: "It's no use, Robert. Don't delay any longer. It's ruining your life. The Lord has called you and you must go."

He turned his face to hers. "Yes, Betsey, it seems so; but how can I take you into this ordeal? How can we leave this home and this land for which we have paid such a price?"

She sat very still, her hand resting on his shoulder as if she were seeing the hard years before them. At last she sat up straight. "I have thought of all these things, oh, so many times. I have dreamed about them at night, and sometimes wept when you were gone. But I have made up my mind, and I am ready."

He looked at her face with astonishment. It was suffused with light such as he had seen in the faces of converts in his revivals.

"We must trust God, that he will keep his word to us," she said. "We cannot see the future, but if we obey, he will take care of us and open the way."

He lifted himself from the rug and threw his arms impulsively about her. "I am not worthy of you," he exclaimed. "We will go."

The decision once made, it was characteristic of them to act without delay—no more hesitancy, no more fruitless misgivings. The determination which had carried him through his brief time at school and the first two years at Shenango came again into positive action. He began arrangements for the care of their property and the steps involved in admission to the conference; she in selecting and packing their personal things in preparation for the journey over the mountains to the East. He probably made some arrangement with his people for the use of his cleared land and the cabin and for sale of the stock, but what they were will never be known.

Candidates for the ministry were required to preach a trial sermon before their local class where their qualifications were known. They might then be recommended for license as a local preacher by the quarterly conference of their own church, or of any charge in the district. They might then be recommended to the annual conference for admission on trial. If accepted, they must remain on trial two years before being ordained as deacon and becoming a member of the conference, and two years more before ordination as elder. Meanwhile, they must be studying in preparation for the work. Thus, it took four years for a young man to become a minister in full standing of the Methodist Episcopal Church.

Roberts' trial sermon was preached in his neighbor Stevenson's cabin. He chose for a text the impassioned prayer of Habakkuk: "O Lord, revive thy work in the midst of the years." He said of this sermon:

> I determined to try to preach let the event be what it might, though I knew not but I should fail. My desire to obtain a license was made known to the society by the preacher, but before they could recommend me they must hear me preach. This was a severe cross but I endeavored to bear it. Whether I preached well or not I cannot say, but the society recommended me.[3]

The venerable Joseph Shane who was present said years afterward: "All present were perfectly amazed; and brother McClel-

[3] *Ibid.*, p. 23.

land, who had been a traveling preacher in Ireland, said to me, 'That is the man. He ought to be in the work. He understands the doctrines of the Gospel well, and is a natural logician.' "[4]

Roberts had next to go to the Holmes Meetinghouse near Cadiz, Ohio, two days' distance by horseback, where Thornton Fleming, the presiding elder, was holding quarterly conference. He says of his experience:

> I understand they had some debating in my case, as I got license by a very small majority as I was so far from home. At the same time I was recommended to travel, for I was determined to go right into the work, as I thought if I could get away from among my friends I could do better.
>
> I went then to Span's neighborhood to hear Brother Fleming preach, but as he did not come it fell upon me as I was the only preacher present. The cross was great and I began with diffidence, every moment thinking the presiding elder was coming in. Then I returned home and began to prepare for traveling though fearful that I would be rejected as I was a married man; but if so my mind would be at rest.[5]

If he were rejected, he might go back to the farm with a clear conscience. He may have hoped he would be rejected.

When Roberts returned to Shenango, he and Elizabeth began preparations for the new life they were entering and for the trip to Baltimore where the General Conference was to meet in April. They were at the same time eager and sorrowful. They did not know when, if ever, they would return to the home which had become dear to them. Their possessions were so few, and what they could take with them on their two horses so little, that the scene would awaken compassion, had it not been heroic.

Robert and Elizabeth sold or gave away the few things of value they could not take with them. They packed garments and bedding

[4] Elliott, *op. cit.*, p. 98.
[5] Simpson ms., p. 25.

in bags for convenience in carrying on the horses' backs, and took along his few books and food for the journey. They literally left all to follow Christ.

Leave-taking at Shenango was difficult; and to many, tearful. Relatives and neighbors from the little valley had come to say good-by. "When I parted from my friends," said Roberts, "it seemed as though it would break my heart and the heart of my wife to leave all our domestic associations and to go forth and be strangers in the wide world." They were like voyagers on an unknown sea. He was not even sure of acceptance at Baltimore and had no slightest inkling of where he would be sent, if accepted.

> But I knew I had only in view the glory of God, the good of the church, and the salvation of my own soul. We traveled over the mountains holding meetings by the way, and I settled my family in York, Pennsylvania, as my wife's mother lived there. This was about three hundred miles.

The arrangement at York was fortunate for them. Elizabeth's father had died, and her mother was glad to have her companionship and assistance in the home. Elizabeth would not be alone during his absences and would have an outlet for her energies during the first trying year.

Chapter IX

Baltimore

LEAVING ELIZABETH AT YORK WITH HER MOTHER, ROBERTS RODE the forty miles to Baltimore. It was his first visit to the Atlantic seaboard. Except for fleeting childhood memories of Maryland he had known only the mountains of western Pennsylvania. Baltimore was a city of twenty thousand inhabitants in 1802, one of the four major centers of population in the young nation. The others were Boston, New York, and Philadelphia. All were seaports and centers of enterprise, and all were growing rapidly. Asbury had made Baltimore his headquarters, and it was the meeting place of the General Conference, so that the city was in effect the national headquarters of the church.

Roberts approached the city with the natural curiosity of a strong mind. He saw for the first time a new kind of forest, the slender masts and spars of pine trees rising from the hulls of ships. Beyond the sea lay the ports from which they came. The first glimpse of the harbor set his mind to thinking of these distant countries. The only ships he had known were the canoes of the Indians and the flatboats and keelboats of the western rivers. He experienced the excitement one feels when coming into a strange city for the first time. He was entering a new and mighty world, strange to him now, but in which he was soon to be at home and to have a place of influence.

Light Street Church, where the Conference was to convene, was on the north side of the business district. It was a substantial building of simple but good design, and had a three-story parsonage on the same lot. The Baltimore Conference, which was a small body of fifty ministers, met on the upper floor of the parsonage. The Conference included southern and western Pennsylvania, Maryland, and Virginia, which then took in West Virginia, and was expanding into eastern Ohio. Francis Asbury presided over its sessions.

Roberts rode up to the church, tied his horse to a hitching post, and entered the building. He was met by one of a committee of laymen, who assigned him to a home for entertainment and arranged for the care of his horse. He met Joseph Shane and James Quinn, the two preachers he knew, and was introduced by them to other preachers, and finally to Asbury. The bishop was kindly, observed him closely, and questioned him about his background, his personal religious experience, and his call to the ministry. Asbury made up his mind quickly that Roberts was a desirable person, but hesitated when he learned he was married. The news that a married man was up for admission had spread rapidly among the ministers, and there was much unfavorable comment.

We have descriptions of the impression Roberts made upon the Conference when it convened the next morning. Abel Stevens writes:

> When he first presented himself in the Baltimore Conference he had traveled thither, from the western wilds, with bread and provender in his saddle-bags and with one dollar in his pockets; but his superior character immediately impressed Asbury and the assembled preachers. He passed in sixteen years from the humble position of a young backwoods itinerant to the highest office of the ministry.[1]

If Elizabeth had been with him in Baltimore when his name

[1] *A Compendious History of American Methodism* (abridged ed.; New York: Phillips & Hunt, 1867), p. 397.

came up for consideration, he would have advised her not to be present during the debate, for things might be said that would hurt her, and she had borne enough already. Word had reached them that one delegate had said to a group: "It were better for him if she were dead." These cruel words would have been disastrous to a woman less resolute than Elizabeth, and they certainly hurt her; but she wanted to know everything and to face the ordeal with him, if there was to be one. As a matter of fact, there was no ordeal. The remarks by those opposed to admission of a married man were considerate. No doctrine of celibacy was at issue, but rather a problem of expediency.

Roberts' admission to the Conference broke the precedent of a quarter century. Soon other itinerants married, and men already married were admitted to the conferences. Their wives invariably faced privations, and several were forced to locate (retire temporarily) to provide for their families. One such case came to Roberts and his wife. John Hall, who preceded him on the Carlisle circuit, resigned and built a powder mill at Shippensburg. The mill blew up, and he was badly injured. His wife implored him not to give up the ministry and urged Elizabeth not to let her husband make the same mistake. Roberts did not think the disaster a judgment upon Hall, but the determination to protect Elizabeth and to secure financial independence began to take form in his mind.

That Asbury liked Roberts and had probably seen Elizabeth is indicated by the considerateness with which he met their difficult situation. He appointed him as junior preacher on the Carlisle circuit. This enabled her to continue to live with her mother during the first year at York, and for her husband to be with her for a few days each month. Asbury was also seeing to Roberts' training by placing him as junior preacher under an experienced man. The senior preacher on the circuit, James Smith, was one of

Asbury's best itinerants; and the presiding elder, Wilson Lee, "a man of great faith, zeal, and usefulness."

The Carlisle circuit had thirty preaching appointments, including Carlisle, Shippensburg, Chambersburg, Gettysburg, Port Royal, Berlin, and points up the Juniata River. It was impossible for every appointment to be on a Sunday, so the preachers carried on during weekdays, leaving announcements of preaching a month in advance, which they always kept. The senior and junior preachers divided appointments, sometimes went together, and helped each other in protracted meetings. The senior preacher directed the work, and the junior preacher was under his supervision and counsel. Asbury, assisted by trusted presiding elders, watched over these preachers closely.

Misfortune overtook Roberts at the beginning of his work. He was taken down with a mild case of smallpox, which fortunately did not leave his face marked; and shortly after with a severe attack of measles, which came while he was out on the circuit. He was cared for by his hosts; not as a burden, but as a privilege, revealing how quickly he was liked. The other misfortune was the death of his two horses. This was a real calamity since he could not make the rounds of the circuit without a horse and had no money to buy one. Somebody loaned him a horse, and later some of the men, who took a liking to him at sight, gave him a mount.

Roberts succeeded as a preacher from the start. He was unassuming, thoughtful, and inspired. His retentive memory was enriched by the finer passages of the Bible. At Little York, which was a Sunday appointment, his reputation spread after his first sermon, and thereafter the community came out to hear him. When he rode up to the church on his second appointment and saw the crowd around the church he could hardly induce himself to enter the building. When he got inside, he found himself facing the leaders of the community as well as his humble Methodist followers; but once begun, he forgot himself in the message.

He proved also to have the gift of an evangelist. People were deeply moved as he preached—moved as he had seen them moved at meetings in his father's house at Ligonier and as he had seen his mother quietly weeping when he sat by her side when James O'Call was preaching. He could hardly understand what was happening, or believe that he, too, had the divine gift. Inspiring revivals which left strong and permanent societies came to points of the circuit.

His first serious difficulty was in meetings where people began shouting, jumping up and down, and falling to the floor. In a way it was a tribute to his eloquence, but these disorderly scenes completely upset him. His early training in the Church of England was shocked by such indecorum in the house of God. He would stop in the midst of a sermon and wait until the excitement subsided. The congregation noticed his embarrassment and were disturbed by his manifest disapproval. Some of the leaders took the matter to the senior preacher.

"We believe Brother Roberts to be a good man," they said, "and we like him well enough as a young preacher, but there is one thing in his course we cannot comprehend. When our meetings become lively, he stops and has nothing to say." Roberts said:

Brother Smith talked with me about it, and I told him their shouting, jumping and falling so confused me that I was not able to proceed. He requested me to keep the reason to myself, saying that if it became known, it would injure me as people would lose confidence in me. Such were my feelings that even once I turned back from the church on a prayer-meeting evening because the noise so greatly confused me. Yet, even at these meetings good was done. At one of our quarterly meetings, probably the second in Carlisle, the meeting-house small, the congregation large, we held meeting in the grove. Our presiding elder commenced preaching (a very neat man, wore a silk gown) and before he closed his sermon such was the effect on the congregation that they were falling in every direction like men in battle. Many professed conversion and crowds went away astonished, wondering what these things could mean.[2]

His first year on a circuit made clear to him and to Elizabeth that he had not mistaken the call, and to Asbury that his judgment about Roberts had been sound. Nevertheless, Asbury gave him another year of instruction and appointed him junior preacher on the Montgomery circuit under Peter B. Davis as senior preacher. This was another vast circuit in the Alexandria district, which extended from Alexandria and Washington to the Ohio River, and from the Pennsylvania line on the north to Charleston and Montgomery, now West Virginia, on the south. It required long patient riding in mountainous country.

Roberts made the first round leaving Elizabeth at York, and looking as he rode the circuit for a suitable place where she could spend the year. He found a room for her in the home of a member at Clarksburg, where she had the privilege of the kitchen. The people were kind to her, as were the people of the church, but her hands were mostly idle. For her husband the year was stirring and eventful, but to her lonely and restless.

Two important friendships, which greatly influenced Roberts' life, were formed during this year. The first was with Nicholas Snethen, traveling companion of Asbury; the other with Philip William Otterbein, gifted and unselfish leader of the German Reformed churches. Both were educated men.

Snethen, who was nine years Roberts' senior, came from Long Island. He was a scholarly man, a linguist, a talented preacher, and a magnetic person. While stationed in Georgetown, he had the friendship of government officials and was appointed chaplain of the House of Representatives. He later broke away from the church on the issue of lay representation and became one of the founders of the Methodist Protestant Church.

[2] Simpson ms., pp. 25-26.

When Asbury learned of Snethen's election as chaplain of the House, he exclaimed in his Journal: "O, great Snethen is chaplain to Congress! So; we begin to partake of the honor that cometh from man. Now is our time of danger. O Lord, keep us pure, keep us correct, keep us holy." [3]

Previous to these occurrences, Asbury had appointed Snethen to accompany him on his long episcopal journeys to share the burden of preaching. On one of these occasions they preached at camp meetings then beginning on the frontier, and Snethen persuaded Asbury to allow one to be started near Baltimore. Snethen had observed Roberts at the Conference and had heard about his revivals on the circuits, so he wrote asking him to announce the camp meeting at his appointments, and invited him to be one of the preachers. Roberts accepted without consulting his senior preacher, which made temporary friction between them; but the trouble ended by Roberst persuading Davis to go along "to see for himself."

At the camp meeting Roberts again met the excesses which had disturbed him the year before. Snethen preached a sermon from the text—"The weapons of our warfare are not carnal, but mighty through God to the pulling down of strongholds." A scene of wild excitement ensued. Roberts was so disturbed that he had two miserable days. He said of the experience, "I had joined the Methodist Church and was now one of its ministers, but it seemed as if I could not endure such scenes."

He resorted to prayer. He went into the woods alone, and like Jacob wrestling with the angel, sought the will of God for himself. The conclusion that he reached was that the work the church was doing was so necessary and effective that he should bear with such manifestations among frontier people as best he could, but should not encourage them.

[3] Ezra Squire Tipple, *The Heart of Asbury's Journals* (abridged ed.; New York: Eaton & Mains, 1904), p. 644.

Roberts' contacts with Otterbein and the German Reformed churches were of a different kind, and were more helpful and congenial to his spirit. Otterbein had come from Moravia and had been educated in Germany. He had assisted at the ordination of Asbury, and his congregations were friendly with the Methodists. These settlers from Germany, which he met with everywhere on his eastern circuits, were a stable and religious people. He remarked to Simpson: "We should have given them more attention, and welcomed their ministers to our conferences and their congregations to our fellowship."

The Baltimore Conference of 1804 sat at Alexandria, Virginia, and met in the month of April. Roberts rode to the conference from Clarksburg where, to his keen regret, he was obliged to leave Elizabeth. The trail led over the high plateau of northern West Virginia into the lovely valley of the Shenandoah River. Spring was breaking on the mountains, and settlers were plowing in the valleys. Redbud and dogwood were in bloom, and hardwoods clothed in light green lay against the darker foliage of the evergreens. It was a pleasant ride except for the thought of Elizabeth waiting alone at Clarksburg.

At this Conference Roberts was ordained deacon by Asbury, assisted by Bishop Coke. This made him a member of the Conference with the right to vote and to the floor. He was given authority, in the absence of elders, to administer the ordinances of Baptism, Marriage, and Burial of the dead, and commissioned "to feed the flock of Christ." Two years later, in regular course, he was ordained elder and fully clothed with the authority and responsibility of a minister of the Methodist Episcopal Church. At present he could not administer the Holy Communion. He was now approaching his twenty-sixth birthday.

Bishop Asbury, by now assured of Roberts, advanced him to the Frederick circuit as senior preacher, with a younger man under his supervision. This circuit extended from near Baltimore to western Maryland, was within a day's ride of Washington, and included Frederick, Maryland, the place of his birth. As soon as he could get away, he hurried back to Elizabeth and brought her east.

An experience on the Frederick circuit gives a picture of the young preacher in action and illustrates how churches got started in those early days. One of Roberts' first appointments was at Harper's Ferry. There was an appointment to preach, but no meeting place and no congregation. But he rode to Harper's Ferry, expecting at the beginning to start a church, however small.

The mistress of the house where he found lodging was a religious woman. When she learned of his mission, she said to him at the dinner table, "Brother Roberts, I want to hear you preach."

He answered, "Sister, I would like to preach for you, but I have no preaching place and no congregation."

She said nothing more and the conversation changed, but when he came back a month later at the hour announced, he entered a house full of women at a quilting party. She removed the frames and said to him, "Now, Brother Roberts, preach for us."

Although surprised, he met the emergency. As has been said, he was a good singer. He had them join in a familiar hymn, and soon they were relaxed by the emotion of the song. Then he preached a sermon the women long remembered. They went back to their homes to tell their menfolk about the preacher, and that night he had a congregation in the same home as the quilting party. When he mounted his horse the following day for the next point on the circuit, he left an organized class and a regular appointment.

The situation of Elizabeth reached a climax at Frederick. The life she was living was no longer endurable to her or to him. She could bear loneliness better than idleness. Loneliness was to be her lot, but not idleness. Their financial resources were also too limited for their needs and for his best work. They had been absent from home three years. They now determined to visit their people and their cabin at Shenango.

They left Frederick in December for the four hundred mile ride. Why they left in winter instead of waiting until the warm months is explained by their determination to get started on the project they had in mind. Every mile of the way was familiar to them. They spent nights with relatives or friends—with her people at York, with his uncle at Bedford, with John at Ligonier. He was asked to preach wherever there were societies, and he no longer hesitated to respond. When they reached Shenango, the whole community welcomed them.

Roberts could remain but a brief time. He had taken a chance in being absent from the circuit for six weeks in the middle of the year. Their plan was revealed when it became known to their people that she would remain at Shenango and that he would go back to Frederick alone. Elizabeth was again happy and like her former self. Work was congenial to her—whether in the house, or the garden, or directing cultivation of their land. She liked to spin and weave and make garments. She was at home again among friends and relatives. She went singing about her work as she put the cabin in order after the long absence. Her husband also fell into his old ways before he left. He mended the roof, rechinked the walls, repossessed a cow and chickens. He took his rifle into the woods and brought back deer and turkeys, stocked the cabin with provisions, and arranged for one of the family to live with Elizabeth during his absence.

He rode back to the Frederick circuit in the coldest part of the winter of 1805; but the cold meant little to his rugged body. His mind was active, thinking of the future and of his work, formulating messages from familiar texts, but he was more at peace about his wife. He had settled upon the farm at Shenango as the answer to security, but how to manage time off was not clear. They must build a larger cabin, the one he had promised her three years before. The community needed a grist mill and he thought about that as a possible enterprise, but he had little capital and might be sent anywhere in the United States. His problems were indeed perplexing, and he could take but a step at a time.

The Baltimore Conference met that spring at Winchester, Virginia. He had an interview with Asbury and laid his plans before him. The bishop was kindly, but gave him no immediate answer; but when the appointments were read on the closing day, he heard his name announced as senior preacher on the Shenango circuit! This gave him his opportunity.

Chapter X

Two Years of Building in the Shenango

THE SHENANGO CIRCUIT INCLUDED CHURCHES AT BUTLER AND Beaver counties, Pennsylvania, four eastern counties in Ohio along the Ohio River, and extended into the Western Reserve. The circuit did not include the society at Shenango, but was near enough to enable Elizabeth to live at home and for Roberts to be with her part of every month. In the middle of the year he was transferred to the Erie circuit which did include Shenango. Here he was kept for a year and a half. These two appointments covered a period of two years and gave him time to carry out his plans for building. He had, of course, to make the monthly round of the circuit and to conduct revival meetings. He also assisted other itinerants on special occasions. But the preachers helped him in return. It was expected, and was so arranged, that a preacher would have a few days at home every month, and a longer period in the summer when men were at work in the fields. These were the free intervals which Roberts could devote to his projects. But he did not hesitate to take more time when needed.

His first undertaking was to build a larger cabin to replace the first one, which had fallen into decay. The new building was sixteen by thirty-four feet. It had two sections divided by a breezeway six feet wide. Each section had a fireplace. The eastern end contained a study and a bedroom, separated by a partition but opening together, and a door from the study into the breezeway. The western end was a common room, sixteen feet square, also opening into the breezeway, and used as a kitchen, dining room, and living room. Here also meetings were held, for as yet the society at Shenango had no church.[1]

Over the eastern end of the cabin was a half-story loft, reached by a ladder from the breezeway and used as a bedroom. Roberts' and Elizabeth's quarters were the eastern rooms. These were small, but gave them privacy. The lower rooms had windows of glass on the south side. The breezeway served also as storeroom and space for the loom.

Fifty feet from the cabin a spring flowed from the hillside into a little pool which the water had hollowed out of the rock. This spring had determined the location of the first cabin. Roberts chiseled a shallow space in the rock for pots and pans, and had built around it stone walls for a springhouse. Above was a small loft for storage of meats and furs.

The gristmill, which was the next undertaking, lay a half mile to the north on Big Run, where the brook fell off steeply into the hollow below. The run is now dry during he summer, but in those days of thick woods it flowed throughout the year. It was only a brook, except at freshets, but the big overshot wheel required little water. Roberts built the dam, the race, and the mill, but he must have employed a millwright to install the machinery. Ruins of the stone dam and the earthen banks of the millrace still remain, but every vestige of the mill has gone. The mill was a convenience to the countryside and prospered as long as Roberts could give it personal attention, but proved unprofitable when he left for Indiana.

Roberts did not attend the Conference in 1807, the first he had missed. He wanted to go to the General Conference, which was

[1] Elliott, *op. cit.*, pp. 146 ff.

to meet in Baltimore in the spring, and felt that he did not have time for both. In his absence charges were brought against him and his junior preacher for neglect of duty, and a vote of censure was passed by the Conference. The two men knew nothing about the action until they received the copy of the resolution from the secretary of the Conference.

The junior preacher, John W. Harris, refused to go to his appointment because of what he felt to be ill-treatment, and located; but he afterward re-entered active work. Roberts accepted the censure. He reasoned with Harris that if they deserved the reproof, the Conference had done its duty; but if not, as they believed, it was their duty to bear it as a cross and not to give up the Lord's work. Nevertheless, the censure rankled. Roberts went to the preacher who presented the resolution and asked him for the evidence of neglect. Charles Elliott who knew the situation considered that the Conference was in error and its action unfortunate.[2]

Although his circuit was large, and the building of his house and mill took all the time he could spare, he found time to advance the church into new territory. On one of these missionary trips he went north toward Erie and Waterford, as far west as Conneaut, Ohio, and as far east as Jamestown, New York. He rode through deep snow on his way to Conneaut, guided by blazes on trees. He spent a cold night in a settler's cabin and slept on the floor with his saddle for a pillow and his feet to the fire for warmth, but was so cold that he slept little. When he came to the house at dusk, only children were at home, but they let him in. When the parents returned, he was made welcome, but the house and the children were smeared with bear's grease. The father had killed a three hundred pound bear the preceding day. They could offer him only fat bear's meat and potatoes, boiled

[2] *Ibid.*, pp. 151-52. Simpson ms., p. 36.

together, and only hay for his horse. He talked with the parents about the religious life of their children, and next morning baptized three of them before he left.

At Lexington he had another experience. He said:

> Three persons professed to get religion some time before under Baptist influence and wanted to be immersed. I had never seen it done. The weather was very cold and though I didn't think it necessary I concluded to baptize them. I hesitated and then went to Conneaut Creek and immersed them. I had to go half a mile to town and my clothes were frozen stiff, but I suffered little inconvenience.[3]

Roberts had a Presbyterian neighbor at Shenango who was building a new house. There was much feeling between the Presbyterians and Methodists in the area, and public debates between their preachers were frequent. The two men were personal friends although divided on religion, and he asked Roberts to "christen" his house when completed, which Roberts consented to do. But meanwhile an unlooked-for incident took place. His neighbor's daughter was converted at a meeting at which Roberts had preached in his own cabin. She went home radiantly happy to tell her family the good news. But her father was incensed, and not being able to change her mind, required her to leave home!

Soon after this happened, his neighbor's house was finished and Roberts was notified that it was ready for dedication. The man seemed to hold no personal grudge against Roberts. When the time came for the formal act of dedication, Roberts preached one of his impassioned sermons. The gathering was carried off its feet, and the following Sunday morning at a meeting held in Roberts' cabin, thirty persons joined the Methodist society, among them the man whose house he had christened.

At the Baltimore Conference of 1808 Roberts was appointed to the West Wheeling circuit as preacher in charge. The circuit included parts of West Virginia, Pennsylvania, and Ohio, and

[3] Simpson ms., p. 33.

was too far distant to be reached from Shenango. Roberts had either to be separated from Elizabeth for a year, or to rent the farm and take her with him. They chose to keep together. One of the Roberts families occupied the house. He took Elizabeth to Cadiz, Ohio, where she found a congenial home with her mother's sister, Mrs. Worley. Here they could be together a few days every month.

When the General Conference met in 1808, it was not as yet a delegated body and every regular preacher had a right to attend. Roberts seemed unusually intent on attending. Probably he was interested in the larger problems of the rapidly growing church, and had already found himself among the leaders. Unhappily, he could not take Elizabeth with him. They had exhausted their savings in their building projects. He had but a dollar in his pocket when he started East, half of which he had borrowed from his junior preacher! There was a man on the way who owed him money, which he hoped to get; but in this he was disappointed.

This Baltimore session proved to be one of the most eventful and dramatic in the history of the General Conference. William McKendree was elected bishop over Cooper and the famous Jesse Lee, by a vote of 95 out of 128 delegates. McKendree was the son of a Virginia planter, a soldier of the Revolution when a young man, and, until his awakening, a communicant of the Church of England in Virginia.

There was no trouble over McKendree, except the personal disappointment of Jesse Lee, which was deep and lasting; but a crisis arose over two issues, which threatened the future of the church. The first was a resolution to make the General Conference a delegated body; the second, a proposal that presiding elders should be elected by the conferences instead of being appointed by the bishop. They were both manifestations of the democratic ferment among the preachers, which, being Americans, was inevitable.

A General Conference composed of all the preachers, and meeting every four years, was expensive and was already becoming unwieldly; but the great objection was that men from the distant conferences were outnumbered by nearby delegates from the East. The Conference of 1808, out of 128 members, had only 2 delegates —Roberts and Shinn—from over the mountains, and 5 from the Western Conference. The New England Conference, anticipating a delegated body, had sent only 7 men.

The issue came up early in the session. The report of the committee appointed to confer on the problem precipitated a long debate and was finally lost. Thereupon the New England delegation and two from the Western Conference arose and requested to withdraw and to go back to their churches. The withdrawal might have resulted in the independence of the annual conferences and a disintegration of the church. Roberts did not participate in the withdrawal of the other preachers from the West. In the emergency Asbury and McKendree met the disaffected delegates privately and persuaded them to return to the Conference. The danger sobered the delegates. The vote was reconsidered and the recommendations of the committee approved. The General Conference of 1812 was therefore to be a delegated body, and the report of the committee contained what became *The Restrictive Rules of the Methodist Episcopal Church,* which are, in effect, a bill of rights. These were drafted by Joshua Soule, a brilliant young preacher and presiding elder from Maine. Soule later was to manage the publishing house of the church, to edit its periodicals, and to be elected to the episcopacy in 1820, the second in order after Roberts.

The division over the presiding elders, which came to the fore at this Conference, was also fundamental. It involved the authority of the bishops to appoint presiding elders, who were selected by the bishops at the sessions of the annual conferences. The opposition proposed election of presiding elders by their conferences, but they were defeated in the balloting. Roberts favored their election and voted with the opposition, but changed his mind under administrative experience. It is clear, however, that he leaned toward democratic principles.

The General Conference of 1808 was a turning point in Roberts' life; not that he was influential in its deliberations, but that it contributed importantly to his training. The problems considered were mainly administrative; but he had a mind for administration, and it was to be his major field of work after 1816.

The more immediate importance of the Conference to him was not related to its sessions, but to his being appointed to preach at Light Street Church on one of the Sundays. That he was asked to preach at the Conference church indicates his growing reputation as a preacher. Light Street was the leading Methodist church in Baltimore. Asbury called it his "Light House."

Roberts was in homespun when he entered the pulpit, but the congregation gave slight attention to his dress when he began to speak. He had a high forehead, an open and expressive face, a magnificent body, and a voice of depth and power. His sermon was on "Pride." He warned the congregation against vanity in dress and luxurious living, and asked in the name of Christ, simplicity and dedication of life to the Christian gospel. The congregation liked the sermon and the preacher, and the next week a committee of laymen waited upon Asbury and asked that Roberts be appointed to Light Street Church. Roberts seems not to have known at the time about their action. Such requests were generally frowned upon. Asbury apparently gave them no assurance at the time but acted six months later.

An amusing sequel to the sermon followed the next week. A leading tailor of Baltimore came to measure Roberts for a suit of clothes! Somebody had noticed his dress, but he never knew who made the gift. One can imagine the surprise of Elizabeth, and doubtless her pleasure, when on his return to Cadiz, she saw him in a well-fitting suit of good English cloth. Did he have the courage to wear it before the homespun congregations of the West? Probably not; but it was to become an appropriate garment within the year.[4]

[4] Elliott, *op. cit.*, p. 155.

Chapter XI

Eight Years in Eastern Cities

THE FUTURE IS OFTEN DETERMINED BY UNEXPECTED EVENTS. Such an event came to Roberts when he was thirty years of age. This was the late fall of 1808. He had been back on the West Wheeling circuit only three months when he received a letter from Bishop Asbury notifying him that he had been appointed to the Light Street Church in Baltimore, and instructing him to leave at once for the charge.

To most of his fellow preachers the appointment would have seemed a golden opportunity, as indeed it was. It proved to be the turning point in his life and of the greatest importance to his future. But to Roberts the assignment brought disappointment to the verge of rebellion. No incident more clearly reveals his character: his lack of the usual ambitions of gifted men, his resoluteness even to obstinancy, his love for frontier life, his loyalty to duty once he saw it clearly, the humilty with which he regarded his own abilities. It is evident from the effect of the letter, that Roberts had not known of the request of the Light Street Church when at Baltimore, and equally clear that he had no ambition for a city pulpit.

He handed the letter to Elizabeth. "Read this letter, Betsey," he said, "it is from Brother Asbury."

When she had finished reading, he continued impulsively, "This is a great mistake. We are not city people, and I am not fitted for such an appointment. Besides, I am in the midst of my year on this circuit, and the work is prospering. How can I leave it so quickly? I am just back from the Conference at Baltimore, and here I am told to return! We have not even money for the journey. If we should go far away from our place at Shenango, and are kept in the East, as we certainly would be, it will ruin our plans for the future. Brother Asbury is a good man, but he has acted hastily and unwisely."

Elizabeth was also disturbed. She, too, was a child of the wilderness and her love for Shenango was as strong as his, but it was not in her to act impulsively. She thought a moment and then said: "You have the ability, Robert. You need not be concerned about that. I have not yet heard a man who is a better preacher. The real question is: does God want you to go?"

This quieted him. They talked on, going over the problems involved. Finally he said, "You are right, Betsey, as you always are. We must pray about it. Meanwhile I will write to Brother Asbury and explain how the appointment looks to us." To which she agreed.

It was a month before Asbury's reply reached them. It was peremptory. "You are always behind," he wrote. "You must come at once to Baltimore. I have appointed another preacher to take your place on the West Wheeling circuit."

Roberts was deeply hurt by the reproach and the peremptory order. "I will surender my parchments," he said in a burst of resentment. "We will go back to Shenango."

But Elizabeth would not consent to such impulsive action. She had made up her mind in the interval between Asbury's letters as to what they should do. She said to him, "Robert, it is your duty to go to Baltimore. Should you return home, you will have greater difficulties than you have ever had before. Bishop Asbury has confidence in you, and it is your duty to obey him. We have already undertaken many difficult journeys, and although we have neither money nor means, we can find a way to get the money. Let us go as soon as possible." [1]

This settled the matter. He had not forgotten his incapacity for effective work during the years of uncertainty about the call to preach. They prepared at once for the trip to Baltimore. They borrowed money, probably from her aunt, Mrs. Worley at Cadiz, Ohio. Their goods were mostly at Shenango, but there was not time to go so far out of the way for them; so they went as they were and reached Baltimore shortly before Christmas.

With this appointment to Light Street Church began eight years in eastern cities—Baltimore, Alexandria, Georgetown, Philadelphia. The farm at Shenango was neglected, as Roberts had foreseen. But, afer his life on the frontier, he could not have been better placed as a preparation for the apostolic labors which followed his consecration as a bishop seven years later. Of course, neither he nor Elizabeth foresaw what was coming.

The cities in which they lived for the next eight years were not the great cities they have since become, but they were relatively as important in the nation's life. Philadelphia was nearing fifty thousand inhabitants; Baltimore, half as many; Alexandria, seven thousand; Georgetown, including Washington, about the same.

The appointment is listed as "Baltimore City" in the minutes of the conference for 1809, and was evidently a circuit in the rapidly growing city, since another charge at Fells Point is mentioned. Assigned with Roberts were two junior preachers, Asa Shinn and Seely Bunn. Roberts took the pulpit of Light Street; Shinn, Fells Point. The importance of the assignment was recognized throughout the communion. It gave Roberts a place among the foremost men of the church.

Hitherto Roberts and Elizabeth had lived on the frontier. They had been in the East from time to time during the previous six years, and had lived at York near Baltimore two years when

[1] Elliott, *op. cit.*, pp. 160-62.

Bishop Robert Richford Roberts

Elizabeth Oldham Roberts. From a portrait in the Bedford, Indiana, Historical Society.

he was on the Carlisle and Frederick circuits; but in habits and speech they were western. For the next eight years they were to be city people and to live in the heart of the nation's life. Both of them made a quick adjustment and were soon at home in the new environment.

Elizabeth found herself living for the first time in a house wholly unlike the rude cabin at Shenango. Old prints show the Light Street parsonage to have been a large and well-constructed building, although in appearance more like a school than a dwelling. "This is the neatest house, within and without, that we have in Baltimore," wrote Asbury in his Journal. It stood originally in the rear of Brydon's dancing hall and was used for dressing rooms. When the hall burned, Asbury bought the entire property, built the Light Street Church over the ruins of the hall, and made a residence and national headquarters of the other building. The third floor was transformed into a conference room by removing partitions and supporting the roof on pillars. An outside stairs led to this floor.

"This room was the scene of many a conference, both quarterly and annual," wrote W. H. Daniels, "and under its rafters for the first forty years of the history of the church, more councils were held, more issues debated, more plans determined, than in any other one house in the whole connection." [2]

The other rooms were living quarters for the minister and his family, and at this time for Seely Bunn who lived with the Roberts. Elizabeth proved a good manager, so effective that the chairman of the Board of Stewards reported that the expenses of the parsonage were half what they were before. She also entered easily into the religious and social life of the congregation. The women liked her and took her shopping with them and into their homes.

[2] *The Illustrated History of Methodism* (New York: Phillips & Hunt, 1887), pp. 513-14.

That Roberts succeeded is shown by the fact that Asbury found a way to send him back the second year. At the end of the first year Asa Shinn was sent to Light Street Church and Roberts to Fells Point down by the harbor; but with the provision that after six months Roberts should return to Light Street and Shinn should take the pulpit at Fells Point. Roberts and Elizabeth meanwhile continued to live at the Light Street parsonage.

His reputation as a preacher is shown by his being asked to preach charity sermons in other than Methodist pulpits. Baltimore, as also Philadelphia, Boston, and New York, had begun charitable institutions which appealed annually to the public through the churches. There is a reference to one such sermon in Washington's diary under date of September 22, 1789, when the Capital was in New York: "Went to St. Paul's Chapel in the forenoon—heard a charity sermon for the benefit of the Orphan's School in this city." [3]

Roberts had learned the meaning of want during his first two years at Shenango and could not forget his sister Elizabeth's assistance to settlers during the hard winter of 1797-98. There was an understanding, a sympathy, an eloquence in his appeals that touched the hearts of listeners and opened their purses.

When his two years at Light Street and Fells Point ended, Roberts could not be kept longer in Baltimore without friction with his fellow ministers. The Conference of 1811, which met in Baltimore on March 20, sent him to the church at Alexandria, Virginia. No junior preacher was appointed with him.

This was another fortunate appointment. Alexandria was a third smaller than Baltimore, but its history reached far back into colonial times. Seagoing vessels tied up at its docks, and Mount Vernon was a two hours' ride to the south. Here Virginia and the southern colonies joined hands with Maryland and the

[3] Benson J. Lossing, *The Diary of George Washington from 1789-1791* (New York: Charles B. Richardson & Co., 1855), p. 55.

North. The lights of the new capital could be seen at night across the flats along the river to the north. Christ Church, where Washington came from Mount Vernon to worship, was in the next block north from the new Trinity Methodist Church.

Roberts and Elizabeth were happy at Alexandria. It was also their introduction to the South. They were living in a comfortable parsonage in one of the famous towns of old Virginia. To the west were the Virginia hills and the near Blue Ridge Mountains over which Roberts had ridden from Montgomery. Alexandria had many homes of old Virginia families, and while the Roberts did not move in these circles, it was an education in taste to live amidst their homes and gardens. The old families knew about them and were kindly, for their rector had exchanged pulpits with Roberts. This rector was William Meade, later third Bishop of Virigina. The Church of England in America had become the Protestant Episcopal Church in 1804, and Roberts, because of his early years in the Church of England, felt at home in its services. Some of the bishops and many of the clergy of the Episcopal Church were friends of Asbury and favorable to the Methodist movement, as was Bishop Meade.

In 1810 Roberts was assigned ot the church at Georgetown, which meant the Capital. Asbury always stopped at Georgetown on his journeys north and south and was a frequent preacher in the church there. Georgetown was the favorite residential quarter of the Capital, so that Roberts had government officials in his congregation. The chief value of the year in Georgetown was his contacts with government. He was soon to become an administrator of large affairs on a national level. He followed the progress of events in Washington with an understanding mind, especially as the War of 1812 approached. However, he had left for Philadelphia before the city was taken.

While in Georgetown, he was one of a group of clergymen who waited upon President Madison. The President had heard about him, and in an aside asked him to call at the White House privately. He was received by the President, apparently more than once. In the first interview Roberts asked before leaving if he might pray with him, to which Madison willingly assented. No great importance can be assigned to these interviews, but they are interesting as related to the impression Roberts made upon people who met him for the first time, and the religious side of President Madison's life.[4]

During the year at Georgetown Roberts took a short trip to Shenango to look after the farm. On his return he brought with him his nephew, George, the six-year-old son of his brother John. He strapped the boy behind him on the horse to keep him from falling off as he took a short cut over narrow trails across the mountains. George was put to school. This is the first intimation that he and Elizabeth were beginning to lose hope of having children of their own. Under the circumstances they did what others have done before and since: they took another mother's child to their hearts and made him their own. His parents doubtless consented so that he might be educated.

In the spring of 1813 Asbury sent Roberts to Philadelphia. Four men were associated with him in the circuit, but William Hunter was preacher in charge. The next year Roberts became the senior preacher, which put him in charge. His pulpit was old St. George's Church, near Independence Hall. The family lived for the next three years in the parsonage adjoining the church. It gave Elizabeth a desirable house at the heart of the city's dynamic life.

The Methodists came into the possession of St. George's Church and parsonage in a peculiar way. The church had been built in 1763 by a German Reformed congregation. It was a large and commanding building, and at the time it was built was the talk of the city. But the congregation became involved in debt,

[4] Elliott, *op. cit.*, p. 163.

and the church was sold at auction. A wealthy young man of feeble intellect, who was looking on at the auction, bid it up to 750 pounds. Later, his father, not willing to expose his son's infirmity, sold it to Captain Webb for the Methodist society for 700 pounds. The original cost had been much greater.[5]

Philadelphia was then a seaport of importance, rich in historical and cultural associations. Here Roberts found colleges, hospitals, libraries, art museums, theaters, printing houses, The American Philosophical Society, The Franklin Institute, and the Academy of Natural Science. The University of Pennsylvania had been in existence sixty years. Independence Hall and the Friends Meetinghouse, and the river with its shipping, were in the same neighborhood. His sensitive ear heard good music. Whatever he may have done to take advantage of these opportunities, they came to him with the air he breathed.

Roberts soon became known beyond his own communion as a public speaker, and in Philadelphia as in Baltimore, was asked to speak in other pulpits in behalf of local charities.

In the fall of 1814 Roberts made an extraordinary and unexpected trip to southern Indiana, a distance of seven hundred miles, going each way on horseback. He was absent four months from his pupit, and no word came from him during that long period. His wife and the church finally became alarmed. The purpose of the journey was, of course known to Elizabeth, but there were dangers on such a trip at the time, and fears of accident or death were natural.

There is but slight record of what led up to the journey. His brother Lewis had gone to Indiana shortly after the battle of Tippecanoe. The valley of the White River and its tributaries had been surveyed and opened for settlement. One may assume that Roberts had sent his brother, and that a report from Lewis

[5] Francis M. Tees, *History of Old St. George's Methodist Episcopal Church.* (Contemporary pamphlet.)

that desirable land at low cost could be secured, had hastened his departure.

On his way from Jeffersonville to Lawrenceport he stopped overnight at Orleans, a half-dozen miles south of Mitchell and near his destination. A company of soldiers stationed there were engaged in target practice. While he was waiting for the stage, he went out to the rifle range and watched their shooting. They noticed him and were told that he was a clergyman from Philadelphia. Thinking he had no knowledge of the rifle and looking for amusement, they challenged him to a trial of skill. Finally Roberts took off his coat, picked up a rifle, and to their astonishment, outshot them all. He did not buy or enter land at this time, but went back three years later with Elizabeth and then bought.[6]

The Philadelphia Conference of 1815 met on the twentieth of April. Bishop Asbury assigned Roberts to the Schuylkill District as presiding elder. The district included Philadelphia, Bristol, Northampton, Dauphin, Lancaster, Chester, and Wilmington. The family continued to live in St. George's parsonage.

He was now to have a year's experience in administration directly under Asbury, valuable training for the following year. A presiding elder was like a suffragan bishop in the Protestant Episcopal Church. He visited each charge at least once every three months, and always preached. He helped his preachers in revivals, watched over their work, counseled the bishop, and directed the general affairs of the church in the area.

The next session of the Philadelphia Conference met on April 18, 1816. Bishop Asbury had died on the thirty-first of March, and Bishop McKendree was greatly enfeebled and could not attend the sessions. In the absence of a bishop, the conferences were instructed to elect a moderator from among the presiding elders. Roberts was elected by a voice vote.

[6] Elliott, *op. cit.*, pp. 65 ff.

Delegates from the New England and New York conferences on their way to the General Conference, which was to meet in Baltimore the next week attended the Conference. They were received with courtesy and invited to the platform. As they watched the proceedings, they were impressed by the dignity and skill with which Roberts presided and put through the business of the Conference.

News of Asbury's death had become known, and it was apparent that the General Conference would have to elect additional bishops. A buzz of discussion about a suitable successor, or successors, to Asbury was going on among the preachers. As the delegates from the North observed Roberts in action, a spontaneous feeling arose among them that he would make a good bishop. They may have talked to members of the Conference, as well as among themselves, but there is no evidence that Roberts knew what was being said. When the agenda reached the election of delegates to the General Conference, Roberts' name headed the list.

Thus ended eight years in eastern cities. When he returned to Philadelphia a month later, the mantle of Asbury rested on his shoulders. He was no longer a member of an annual conference, but the highest official in the gift of the church, responsible alone to the General Conference. He and Elizabeth had come from the frontier, but when they left, they were as much at home in Philadelphia as in Shenango. They were wilderness people become cosmopolitans. Their horizons had greatly expanded and their minds had been vitalized by the currents of thought so powerful at the time in those cities. They could go back to the wilderness without losing what they had gained. Roberts, as if prepared by Providence, was ready for his apostolic labors.

Chapter XII

Bishop Roberts

THE GENERAL CONFERENCE OF 1816 WAS OVERSHADOWED BY the death of Bishop Francis Asbury. He was on his way to the Conference with his traveling companion, John Bond, from a long episcopal journey in the southern states. He was so weak during the journey that he had to be carried from the pulpit when he insisted on preaching. As he neared Fredericksburg on his way from Richmond, he became so ill that Bond turned off the direct road to the home of Asbury's friend, George Arnold, at Spotsylvania. Here he died on the thirty-first of March. They laid him to rest in the Arnold family burying ground, and Bond came on to Baltimore to bear the sad news to the Conference.

Asbury had directed the destinies of the Methodist societies in America for over forty years. He had been sent to America by Wesley in 1771, along with others of Wesley's preachers, and had quickly come into leadership. As the struggle with England developed in intensity and bitterness, he was forced into retirement for two years at the home of his friend Judge White of Delaware. But when it was realized that he had cast his lot with the colonies, he was allowed to resume his work.

Asbury was consecrated the first bishop of the Methodist Episcopal Church at the Christmas Conference in 1784. Although appointed general superintendent by Wesley, he refused to act as such until elected by the preachers of his adopted country. When this was done, and unanimously, he had no more hesitancy.

He selected the presiding elders, appointed the preachers to their circuits, and directed the affairs of the church like a general commanding an army. He asked and received the necessary grants of power because of his great administrative ability, and because he was loved and trusted. From the time he came to this country he kept a record of what he did. He preached 16,500 sermons, ordained above 4,000 preachers, and traveled 270,000 miles, mostly on horseback. He visited the South thirty times in thirty-one years. His journal is replete with references to illness, fevers, and infections of the throat due to constant speaking and exposure; but he nevertheless kept on with his prodigious labors.

When the General Conference assembled at Baltimore on the first of May, they were like sheep without their shepherd. The old order was passing before their eyes. But they were self-reliant men, accustomed to emergencies, and confident of divine guidance. The Conference voted at its first session to bring the body of Asbury to Baltimore for interment in the Eutaw Street Church. A committee was sent to Spotsylvania for the purpose.

The committee came back on the fifth of May, and on the ninth a memorable service was held in the Light Street Church, where the Conference was sitting. The venerable Bishop McKendree, William Black—the representative of British Methodism—John Bond, and Henry Boehm—Asbury's surviving traveling companions—followed by the delegates of the General Conference, the clergy of all faiths, and a large concourse of citizens, moved through the streets of Baltimore to the Eutaw Street Church. After a memorial service addressed by McKendree, the body was placed in a crypt beneath the altar.

"Asbury's remains rested in the vault of Eutaw church until June, 1854, when they were again disinterred and finally deposited in Mount Olivet Cemetery in Baltimore, . . . And there Methodism's greatest itinerant hero sleeps his last sleep." [1]

[1] Tipple, *op. cit.,* p. 712.

Asbury was an extraordinary man. He had exceptional insight in selecting personnel, the gift of command, and a devotion so manifest that the preachers followed him willingly. He won the personal friendship and support of many of the leading men of his day—men like governors Tiffin and Livington, Judge White, and Bishop Meade. They were glad to have him in their homes and contributed generously to his projects although many of them were not affiliated with his societies. James M. Buckley speaks of

> the consummate wisdom of Francis Asbury, fully equal to that of John Wesley, . . . No general ever stationed his troops with greater skill than Asbury displayed in the adjustment of ministerial supplies to the infant societies. He knew whom to trust, and, ceaselessly moving among the people, made changes without regard to the limitation of time, composed feuds by authority and counsel, rekindled dying interest or quenched the flames of fanaticism, extricated a brother from the consequences of his own imprudence, or delivered a society from the control of an indiscreet administrator.[2]

When the Conference assembled after the funeral, a committee was appointed to bring in a report on the episcopacy. Bishop McKendree, the only surviving bishop, was failing. After deliberating, the committee advised the election of two bishops. The Conference began balloting on the morning of the fourteenth of May. There were no nominations, but each delegate voted for the man he thought best fitted for the high office. The conference had 105 delegates, 100 voting, a majority being necessary for election. On the first ballot Enoch George received 57 votes and was declared elected. On the second ballot Robert Richford Roberts received 55 votes and was elected. George was a North Carolinian, presiding elder of the Potomac District; Roberts, presiding elder of the Philadelphia District.

The effect upon Roberts of his election was characteristic.

[2] *A History of Methodism in the United States* (New York: The Christian Literature Co., 1897), II, 268.

During the interval between his election and his consecration he had great mental conflict as to his duty. There seemed to have been no elation, such as might have been expected, but rather depression. He questioned his own fitness for the office, and was uncertain whether he should consent to ordination. In his perplexity he turned to Elizabeth and to his old friend, James Quinn. They finally persuaded him that it was his duty to accept. Quinn said that Roberts wanted to be sure that it was the will of God.

Two days later, on the sixteenth of May, the two men were consecrated. What must have been Roberts' emotions when he found himself kneeling at the altar of his old church in the solemn ceremony of ordination, the venerable Bishop McKendree and the presbyters laying their hands one over the other upon his head, the familiar church crowded with the delegates to the General Conference, his old friends from Baltimore, and Elizabeth watching the ceremony.

James Quinn said long afterward, alluding to the decision of the New York and New England delegates to support Roberts:

> When we of the west heard this, we were surprised and could scarcely believe the report. But we soon found that they were in good earnest about the matter, and that New York and New England men would most willingly go with the Philadelphians, for his election to the episcopal office. We heartily approved of the promotion of our fellow backwoodsman, and rejoiced to hear of the event, unexpected though it was. Thus, fifteen years after I heard him deliver his first exhortation, I saw him placed in the episcopacy by the election of the General conference and the ordination of Bishop M'Kendree. Though elevated to the most important office in the Church, he still retained the character of being a modest, unassuming man.[3]

Bishop Roberts entered at once upon the duties of his office. The next morning Roberts occupied the chair, as he did frequently the remainder of the session. Bishop George was not

[3] Elliott, *op. cit.*, p. 167.

in the chair during the Conference. Bishop McTyeire comments: "His feeling of self-distrust was such as to make the duties of public intercourse, which his office drew upon him, embarrassing and painful. For constitutional questions he had no taste."[4] The transition from his former status was so precipitate that it might well have been disconcerting: but, contrary to his hesitancy before ordination, he began with the competence and assurance of an experienced moderator. He had an exceptional memory, knew the names and faces of delegates, was familiar with parliamentary procedure, presided with dignity and fairness, understood points at issue in debates quickly, and seldom made decisions which were protested or reversed.

Roberts and Elizabeth had little time to make plans for the future. Within a week after the close of the General Conference he was on his way to New York to hold the New York Conference, which met on June 1. From New York he met the New England Conference on June 22 at Bristol, Rhode Island. Elizabeth remained in Philadelphia. She was not alone as she had been when her husband was riding the circuit. She was among friends in an interesting city, and had with her their nephew George.

The family continued to live in St. George's parsonage until they could determine where to establish their permanent residence. No bishop's palace was provided for a Methodist bishop. He must live humbly, like his brethren, but he was free to choose his own residence. As soon as Roberts returned to Philadelphia, they faced this problem. They had no time to lose, since the fall conferences were coming on when he must again leave for distant places.

This was the third time they had experienced a radical change in their affairs: the first when they gave up their plans at Shenango for an itinerant life; the second when they left the frontier for

[4] Holland N. McTyeire, *A History of Methodism* (Nashville and Dallas: Publishing House of the Methodist Episcopal Church, South, 1910), p. 537.

Baltimore; now the most unexpected and difficult of all. But the situation had two great advantages: they could live where they pleased; and, within the limitations of a bishop's rigorous life, they could resume their plans for independence. It was the more important that they should do so because of the demands that were sure to be made upon his slender resources.

Three choices seemed to be open to them. They might make their home in Baltimore or Philadelphia where they had many friends. The church would welcome the decision, but it was ruled out because of the expense of living in such a place. The salary of a bishop was only two hundred dollars and traveling expenses, and a small allowance for his family. Asbury had fixed the amount based upon his own single and rigorous life. Roberts' pride and the memory of the cruel words about a married preacher when he entered the Conference led him to refuse the family allowance until three years later.

The second alternative was for Elizabeth to travel with him. But this was manifestly impracticable. What should they do with George, who had become dear to them? He had taken the place of the child they had hoped for. The bishop could not ask her to take the long journeys on horseback to the ends of the nation, which was to be his lot; nor could he ask for entertainment in private homes, often unexpected, without embarrassment. Besides, she should again be living a life of idleness and futility. The final decision made itself. They would go back to Shenango, at least for the present, until they could decide about Indiana.

Another factor influencing the decision was less personal. Roberts saw more clearly than other leaders after the death of Asbury that the future of the church lay in the Mississippi Valley, and that one of the two new bishops should make his episcopal residence in that region. McKendree was in failing health, George was eastern and chose to live in Washington, Roberts was western and was clearly the one to go.[5]

Once the decision was made, he acted quickly. He closed his affairs at Philadelphia and prepared for the journey to Shenango. Friends in Baltimore bought Asbury's team of horses, his enclosed carriage and traveling trunk, and presented them to Bishop Roberts. The Robertses packed what they could take with them and set out on the journey.[6]

They reached the old home at Shenango in early August, and found the house and outbuildings badly in need of repairs after their eight years' absence. He could do but little to restore the buildings since he must leave in September for the Mississippi Conference at Natchez, but he did what he could. He fell quickly into his old ways. The spirit of adventure and the love of the wild came back to him. He found time to take his rifle into the forest and brought back deer and wild turkeys. His skill with the rifle had not left him. He was happy to be working again with his hands and experienced a resurgence of physical energy upon which he was to draw heavily during the months to come.

[5] Asbury to McKendree: "I told him my opinion was that the Western part of the empire would be the glory of America for the poor and pious; that it ought to be marked out for five Conferences, to wit: Ohio, Kentucky, Holston [Tennessee], Mississippi and Missouri." Tipple, *op. cit.*, p. 699.

[6] As Asbury became more infirm, friends in Philadelphia had given him a covered carriage in which he could travel with more comfort. (*Ibid.*, p. 674.) This was the carriage bought by Roberts' friends. Asbury's traveling trunk, which they also bought and presented to Roberts, was a small wooden box with lid and handle, and was covered with deerskin, with the hair on the outside. Roberts used this on his travels to hold his papers. When he died, Mrs. Roberts gave the trunk and her husband's papers to the Indiana Conference, and the Conference entrusted them to the Indiana Asbury University at Greencastle. Here in some way they passed into private hands and were again apparently lost. I found the trunk in 1952 in a cabinet of Indian artifacts, and placed it for permanent keeping in the University archives, but the invaluable papers have disappeared.

Chapter XIII

Journey to Natchez—1816

BISHOP ROBERTS' STAY AT SHENANGO WAS BRIEF. THREE MONTHS after his ordination on May 17 he began preparations for the long journey into the South. He was to meet the Mississippi Conference at Natchez on October 10, the South Carolina Conference at Columbia on Christmas Day, the Virginia Conference at Petersburg on February 5, the Baltimore Conference at Baltimore on March 12. The journey was to take him away from home seven months, over a distance of four thousand miles, mostly along the fringes of civilization much along Indian trails, and every foot of the way on horseback. What an introduction to his high office! [1]

The prospect of the long absence of her husband, the manifest danger to him, and her loneliness, would have been insupportable to Elizabeth but for her patience and her own dedication. She clung to him as the day approached for his departure, and finally decided to ride with him as far as the home of her aunt at Cadiz,

[1] In the Introduction I have made reference to the fact that Roberts kept no journal. In the absence of such a source I have searched for information in the minutes of the conferences over which he presided and in histories of these conferences. The Rev. John G. Jones, who was present at the Conference in Natchez in 1816, wrote *A Complete History of Methodism as Connected with the Mississippi Conference of the Methodist Episcopal Church, South* (Nashville: Southern Methodist Publishing House, 1887), in which Ch. xix of Vol. I is devoted to Bishop Roberts' visit. This chapter is rich in descriptions of the bishop's personality, his preaching and his methods of work, concerning which there is a scarcity of material. I have, therefore, used it extensively in this chapter.

Ohio, and back alone the hundred miles to Shenango, just to have the few extra days with him. When they reached Cadiz, he could not delay beyond a single night, for he was already late. With a heavy heart she saw him disappear the next morning over the Ohio hills.

The distance to Natchez was roughly a thousand miles. The route lay across Ohio and Indiana to Louisville, through Kentucky to Nashville, then over the Natchez Trace six hundred miles to Natchez, most of the way but a bridle path. He had only one horse for the journey. He left Shenango the last week in August and was a day late at Natchez on October 10, so that the trip took between six and seven weeks. If Roberts averaged thirty miles a day, he made good time.

Roberts reached Natchez in the fall of 1816. The Battle of New Orleans had been fought the year before. When he reached Port Gibson, he passed out of the wilderness into fairly settled country, and at Natchez found himself in a city as old as Philadelphia.

The Mississippi Conference met on October 10 at the home of William Foster at Pine Ridge, seven miles north of Natchez. Foster was a prosperous planter, and the men of the Conference were guests in his house. He and his wife, Rachel, were converts of Lorenzo Dow. They had been Methodists for seventeen years and considered it a privilege to entertain the Conference.

The Conference was given one of the upper rooms for its sessions. The preachers also used it as a common bedroom. There were only seven of them in addition to Bishop Roberts. The large living room on the first floor was used for preaching services and ordination of elders and deacons. The preachers took their meals with the family. They were a happy company, both hosts and guests, the preachers relaxing from a year of isolation, Roberts from his thousand mile ride from Pennsylvania.

Why did the bishops think it worth while to send one of their number so far to meet such a small number of preachers? Why might not the Conference have been left to manage its own affairs, for which they were always prepared? The answer is that this was the session for organization of the Conference, which required the presence of a bishop. But the greater reason was that the bishops, especially Roberts, saw the future of the region. The Conference included Mississippi and Alabama south of the Tennessee River and all of Louisiana south of the Arkansas River. This vast territory was filling with settlers. They were coming up the Mississippi and its tributaries, down through Tennessee from the valley of Virginia, and across Georgia and Alabama. Roberts had had enough experience with the great migration to foresee that this little band of preachers would multiply manyfold.

Roberts was a day late at the Conference, as might well have been expected because of the length of his journey. However, when asked what delayed him, the bishop answered laconically, "I didn't start in time."

The historian of the Conference wrote:

> Most hearty and joyous was the greeting between them and the first Bishop (of their race) that ever put his foot on Mississippi soil. Tommy Owens [a lively Irishman], especially, was in ecstasies. For the first time in his earthly existence he had seen a live Bishop. The privilege of being introduced to the Bishop, and being called by him "Brother Owens," he felt was the greatest honor of his life. . . . None enjoyed the arrival of the Bishop more than Mr. and Mrs. Foster, . . . For seventeen years they had been striving to serve the Lord, and to assist in building up the church of their choice amidst the surrounding darkness and wickedness.

Roberts took the chair at two o'clock and presided over the remaining sessions. He brought the conference $499.06¼ from general funds, to be devoted to supplementing the salaries of the preachers. Of the amount, $30.00 went toward Roberts' expenses and $20.00 to Bishop McKendree. How they arranged the quarter penny is not explained.

There was preaching every day at noon by some member of the Conference. Bishop Roberts preached for the first time on Saturday. He chose for his text Heb. 12:1: "Seeing we also are compassed about with so great a cloud of witnesses." They were emotionally tense, and Roberts spoke with feeling. Thomas Nixon, one of the preachers, recorded in his diary that two thirds of the congregation were in tears. On Sunday the bishop preached twice to a congregation which had come in from the surrounding country. At the ordination of deacons he preached from Jer. 9:23-24:

"Thus saith the Lord, Let not the wise man glory in his wisdom, neither let the mighty man glory in his might, let not the rich man glory in his riches: but let him that glorieth glory in this, that he understandeth and knoweth me, that I am the Lord which exercise lovingkindness, judgment, and righteousness, in the earth: for in these things I delight, saith the Lord."

This and subsequent texts, which Jones is careful to list and often quotes, together with descriptions of the bishop's preaching and effects upon audiences, give rare pictures of Roberts in the pulpit. His sermons were thoughtful and carefully organized, but also highly emotional. Jones uses the term *pathetic,* in a sense now obsolete, to mean, "with deep feeling, eloquent." Audiences were greatly moved, often to tears, and there were many conversions.

When the assignments of preachers had been announced at the closing session and the Conference adjourned, Bishop Roberts made a two weeks' tour of the churches with his preachers instead of leaving at once for the next conference at Columbia, South Carolina, which he might have been expected to do. Word was sent in advance of his coming, and he preached at Natchez, Washington, Midway, and more distant settlements. He was not able to get to the only circuit in Louisiana across the Mississippi toward Alexandria, because of high water. The settled country in Mississippi was within a radius of twenty miles of Natchez, except toward Port Gibson which he visited on the way north.

The preachers and their bishop spent Monday night after adjournment with their hosts, the Fosters. On Tuesday they rode to Natchez. Roberts made purchases of books and other needed articles, and left an appointment to preach on Wednesday. He also rode about the old Spanish town and watched traffic on the great river. He saw flatboats from the Ohio, such as he had known at Pittsburgh, floating slowly toward New Orleans. He may have seen the third steamboat ever to ply the river, which in 1816 was carrying passengers and freight between Natchez and New Orleans. The first river steamer on the Mississippi had passed Natchez four years before.

The Jones narrative continues:

Friday night, they spent with a Mr. Sojourner; dined on Saturday with a brother Hodges; and spent the night after their fatiguing ride in comfort with Mr. Richardson near Midway. The next day, the people flocked out from all the region around about to hear the bishop, whose fame had preceded him on the return of William Winans—who lived in the neighborhood—from the late conference. In those days, when "the word of the Lord was precious," where two preachers met, especially at a Sabbath service, the people expected to hear a sermon from each. Moreover, as this was Mr. Lane's circuit, the people would like to hear their new preacher. The bishop therefore requested Mr. Lane to preach first, and he would follow.

Mr. Lane preached from I Peter 2:4, and the bishop took his text from John 1:29: "Behold the Lamb of God, who taketh away the sin of the world." The congregation was very attentive, and seemed to be deeply interested throughout the protracted service. An old gentleman who had failed to get the order of the day, when he saw Mr. Lane, with his manly form and commanding physiognomy rise up in the pulpit doubted not that he was the bishop. The old gentleman was all attention and admiration. When Mr. Lane concluded, another fine looking preacher, apparently beyond the middle of life, rose up and delivered a very intelligent and feeling sermon in the most perfect style of pulpit oratory. After dismissal, the old gentleman, quite elated with the sermons, said to a friend that the bishop preached an admirable sermon, but that he believed the old gentleman that followed rather beat the bishop.

On Monday, Roberts preached at McCalley's church, from Proverbs 22:11: "He that loveth pureness of heart, for the grace of his lips the King shall be his friend." On Tuesday he preached at Liberty the county town of Amite. Here he was taken sick, but he rode eleven miles after preaching on his way to Franklin County. On Wednesday morning, he appeared much better, and with his traveling companion rode twenty-eight miles to Pickett's. The Pickett settlement was then one of the strongholds of Methodism in Franklin County. All the elder Picketts—both men and women—so far as we know—belonged to the church. No doubt the bishop intended to preach in the neighborhood but on the morning after his arrival he had a protracted chill which was followed by fever that confined him to bed the most of the day. Having other engagements ahead he rode six miles in the evening to Mr. King's where he spent a rainy night. They left early next morning and rode thirty miles to Rev. Randall Gibson's, eight or nine miles south of Port Gibson. The bishop's confinement to bed so late the day before put them so much behind they did not get to Mr. Gibson's in time to fill an appointment made for him that day.

Here Bishop Roberts had a severe spell of sickness—chills and fever. He was so ill on Monday, the 28th, that Mr. Gibson sent to Port Gibson for Dr. Thomas Going. The doctor afforded him great relief and predicted an early recovery. In the evening, he was much better, came downstairs, and spent a short time in cheerful conversation with the family. Mr. Nixon, his traveling companion, made some allusion to the vast circuit in the Attakapas country to which he had been appointed by the bishop—a circuit filled with as many natural and moral difficulties and dangers as were ever crowded into a country of the same extent. The bishop replied, "When a general has a dangerous outpost to guard he sends to the point of danger his most trustworthy officers, and they should feel honored by the appointment." Mr. Nixon appreciated the allusion and assured the bishop that he would guard that dangerous post to the best of his ability. Nixon's forecast of hardship on his circuit were not overdrawn.

The conference historian tells of another of the preachers, John Shrook, who had come up from Alexandria, Louisiana, where he had recently introduced Methodism by preaching in the courthouse. He had antagonized the rough element by denouncing their evil ways and had been threatened with violence. "We will duck him in the Red River," the young men were saying about town. Shrook had been a blacksmith before his conversion. When the time came for the service, he walked through the crowd in front of the courthouse with his coat off and the butt of a loaded whip in his hand and invited them to come in and hear him preach. Walking up to the judge's bench, he laid his saddlebags and whip across the table, rolled up his sleeves, flexed his strong arms, opened his collar revealing his thick neck, and warned them.

Nothing happened, but what he did was noised about the country, and when he came up to the Conference, he was asked by his admiring brethren to tell about the incident. This he proceeded to do with manifest pride, evidently to the pleasure of the preachers. When he had finished, Roberts, who had been listening quietly, turned to Shrook and said only, "Peter, put up thy sword." The words were kindly spoken, but the effect upon the Conference was immediate and sobering. It was as if they heard the Master speaking to his impetuous disciple in the Garden of Gethsemane.

Jones, writing in summary of the tour of Roberts among the Mississippi churches, concludes:

> This is all we know about our first episcopal visitation in Mississippi. Here the curtain falls, and what next happened to our greatly admired and highly esteemed bishop we have no means of knowing.

Tradition says that his stay at Mr. Gibson's was protracted on account of the extreme debility which succeeded his violent illness. As he did not return to his home until early in the following spring, we assume he went from here to the South Carolina Conference, and to several other conferences further eastward on the Atlantic slope.

We know definitely that he lay ill for a month at Randall Gibson's home—and for a time critically ill—and that he received skillful and gentle care. If Elizabeth had known of his condition she would have been frantic. He left for Columbia, South Carolina, before his strength had returned, and had a relapse among the Indians of Mississippi through whose lands he journeyed. They gave him sour hominy to eat, probably all they had, and overcharged him at ferries until they learned that he was a great chief of the white men. This incredible seven-hundred-mile winter ride of the sick man, through the worst wilderness in the United States to keep an engagement, witnesses to his character. He reached Columbia in time for the opening of the Conference on Christmas Day.

When he had finished with the South Carolina Conference, he was not so pressed for time and could ride more leisurely. His next conference was the Virginia one at Petersburg on February 5. He was now traveling in a country which had been settled for a hundred years. He followed the route taken by Lord Cornwallis from the Carolinas to Yorktown. From Petersburg he rode to Alexandria and Georgetown. Here people thronged his former churches to hear him preach and to listen to accounts of the work in Mississippi. From Washington he rode the forty miles to Baltimore in a single day. One can imagine his welcome by the Baltimore Conference and by the people of the Light Street Church. The preachers were interested in the new conference in Mississippi and in the progress of the work in the South. Everybody wanted to hear about his experiences in that faraway country, and especially when it became known how ill he had been.

Finally, he set his face homeward. The autumn of 1816, the winter of 1816-17, and the first month of spring had passed since he had said good-by to Elizabeth at Cadiz. He was tired and ill, and his faithful horse was in need of rest. The miles dragged as he rode along the familiar route which he and Elizabeth had ridden so often. She, too, was waiting, he knew, she and the boy George; for he had written her to expect him.

Elizabeth had gone back from Cadiz to Roberts' sister Nancy's home the previous August, but in the late fall she had wearied of living in another's house and had returned with George to their own cabin. Her brothers-in-law had helped her repair the roof and bring in wood and supplies, and she had then passed the lonely months with greater contentment. But when she saw his familiar figure approaching the house, she ran out to meet him and wept on his shoulder. She was shocked when she saw his face yellowed with jaundice. Malaria was again upon him. He even allowed her to unpack his saddlebags and care for the big bay horse, an unheard-of thing to do in other days. She brought out clean linen, arranged a bath, and put him to bed. Then she brought food and let him sleep. Time to talk after he had awakened and the restorative processes had begun.

Chapter XIV

Move to Indiana

A HEAVY RAIN FELL THE NIGHT HE ARRIVED, AND HE WAS completely soaked from a leaking roof while asleep. He awakened with a chill followed by fever, and the jaundice grew worse. His recovery was slow, and the four months before the fall conferences began were none too long to regain his strength. But under Elizabeth's care and good food he grew better. He lived mostly out-of-doors, began to work about the house and farm, hunted a little, and by September was again ready for the saddle.

When the bishop and his wife came from Philadelphia in the summer of 1816, they had settled upon Shenango as their permanent home; but the long journey to the South convinced him that the future of the church lay much farther west and south, and that Shenango was too far north for the work he had to do. It was near the Canadian border, at the foothills of the Allegheny Mountains and on the eastern border of the Mississippi Valley. Southern Indiana was better located for his episcopal duties. It was near the Ohio and Wabash rivers and accessible to all parts of the country.

But he had other and more personal reasons. The soil at Shenango was not as fertile as he had thought it to be. Southern Indiana was a bluegrass country, the growing season was longer, and land was plentiful and cheap. It is evident from what he did that he was also concerned about the future of relatives, especially the young people. There was a chance for them in

Indiana. Then, too, Indiana was on the frontier, and the frontier was always calling him.

His brother Lewis was at Bono on the White River, and they were writing back and forth; but we know little except by inference of the long and anxious discussions which led to the final decision to move to Indiana. It must have seemed to Elizabeth that they should always be moving and that she should never have a settled home. What is known is that when the fall conferences of 1817 were over, he and Elizabeth made a quick trip to Lawrence County, Indiana, for her to see the country and to inspect the land he had in mind. They traveled on horseback and took the southern route to the falls of the Ohio, and then the Vincennes Trace to Mitchell.

This extra trip of six hundred miles to Indiana with Elizabeth is important to an understanding of his character and his personal relations with her. Most men of the time would have made the decision themselves and avoided the journey, or taken it in connection with an official duty. But he and Elizabeth were comrades and were working together, and it was only fair, he thought, that she see for herself before committing her life to another frontier experience. The heavy burdens of isolation and physical labor would fall mainly on her. She would have to manage the farm during his long absence. She had a gift for management, which he well knew and upon which he must rely; but the isolation must be voluntary.

After riding over the area with his brother Lewis, they selected a tract of land in the extreme southeast corner of Lawrence County. It lay among the hills five miles southwest of Bono. The village of Lawrenceport was not then in existence. He could hardly have found a more out-of-the-way place, but it suited his mood and his pocketbook. Asbury had dubbed him "Mountain Roberts" to distinguish him from George Roberts, another preacher of the same name. Surely only a mountain-bred man would have selected this hill country. But it was good land and in the most beautiful part of Indiana. Bono was an ambitious community from which produce was already being shipped by flatboat down the White River to New Orleans. From his experience at Shenango where he could sell nothing but pelts and furs Roberts knew the importance of accessibility to markets.

A small stream called Fishing Creek ran through the land he bought, providing running water and bottom fields. The country to the north was gently rolling and promised well. All was covered with magnificent poplars and hardwoods. They selected a site for a cabin near the foot of a hill sloping towards Fishing Creek and overlooking its little valley. The place was hidden in woods, but had charm and scenic beauty. The location of the cabin was determined by a spring which flowed from a limestone cliff on the western face of the hill. A hundred feet north was another larger spring which poured out of the rock. The site of this first cabin, which was built by Lewis before their coming, is still marked by stones from the chimney and a cavity where a cellar was dug.

Having bought the land and fixed the location of the cabin, they rode back to Shenango; but nearly two years elapsed before he could arrange his affairs and find time from the pressure of episcopal duties. He should need at least four months to make the journey and to get settled before he could safely leave Elizabeth and the children, their twelve-year-old nephew George and fourteen-year-old Esther, daughter of his beloved sister Elizabeth.

His schedule of conferences in 1818 was unusually heavy: The Virginia, February 26 at Norfolk; the Baltimore, March 26; the Philadelphia, April 22; the New York, May 14; the New England at Hallowell, Maine, June 4; the Genesee at Lansing, Cayuga County, New York, July 16. These were six out of the eleven conferences of the church. McKendree and George took the five western and far southern. The Mississippi that year fell to Bishop

McKendree and was held in the home of John Ford at Sandy Hook on the Pearl River. McKendree was so ill and the Conference so small that the sessions were held in the bedroom while he lay propped up with pillows.

Roberts was absent from home six months on this round of conferences. The labor was exacting, but involved much less exposure and danger from sickness than the previous year. His travels were mostly in a settled country with good inns and comfortable homes. He had one night out when he lay with his head on the saddle and held the lead rope of the horse while he slept. He had also three days without food, except wild berries, when he rode from the Genesee Conference through southern New York to Shenango. He probably ran out of money and was unwilling to ask for food when he could not pay for it. But to do without food was not a new experience.

In January of this same winter Mrs. Roberts made a trip to the eastern cities where they had lived for eight years. They had evidently been happy years or she would not have ridden the nine hundred miles in winter to visit them again. She was homesick to meet her friends once more before leaving for the distant West, knowing well that she might never see them again. So far as is known, she never did. They had also been obliged two years before to leave behind at Baltimore clothing, books, and presents from friends, and she wanted to take them back with her. She had expected to have company on the journey, but this failing, she went on alone as far as Bedford, Pennsylvania. From Bedford she had company to Alexandria. What a picture of this pioneer woman!

The Virginia Conference finished, Roberts joined her there. He had a month before the opening of the Baltimore Conference, but not a month of idleness, for he had much correspondence and speaking. He preached at Alexandria and Georgetown, and there were dinner parties in their honor. The Roberts were good hosts at home and equally pleasant guests. He was friendly and humorous and had a fund of interesting experiences. She took her part in the conversation about tables and firesides, as she did at home.

From Georgetown they rode to Frederick and York where they had lived as children and where each had relatives. From York they rode to Baltimore and then on to the Philadelphia Conference. This gave them six weeks among old friends who greatly liked and honored them. They were constantly invited out. She visited and shopped with the women, and bought new garments for the children to take with her to the West.

Such times always end too soon, but they leave memories that are good to live with. The bishop had to meet the New York Conference on May 14, and she had to ride back to Shenango alone. They bought an extra horse for her journey and loaded the two animals with their purchases. She went as far as Pittsburgh with a young man and his wife, and then rode on alone the remaining miles to Shenango. Her husband returned two months later.

Another year elapsed before they could get away. It must have seemed to them sometimes as if they would never get started. He probably took the Ohio, Missouri, and Tennessee conferences in the fall of 1819. It seems likely that he met the Ohio Conference at Cincinnati on August 7, the Missouri at Cape Girardeau on September 14, the Tennessee at Nashville on October 1; and then hurriedly returned to Shenango for the long-awaited move to Indiana.

They finally started the first week in November of 1819. The bishop had planned an early start the day they left, but the people of the valley came to see them off. Their friends brought food for the journey, and there were good byes, and tears, and prayers by the local preachers Gurwell and McClelland, but finally they were off.

They took along George, Esther, and two young men, Thomas and Robert, sons of his brother Thomas. They had two horses for the carriage and two for riding. Esther rode one of the horses, with George either behind her or riding in the carriage with his uncle and aunt. The two young men alternately rode the other horse and walked. The carriage was packed with baggage, and the saddle horses carried packs. They took along everything they could possibly carry, for they would need much more than they could take with them. They spent the first two nights out with friends, but after that stopped mostly at inns. These were rough log houses where they could get shelter and provender for the horses, but often in good weather they camped out and had their meals by the roadside. To the children and the young men it was an exciting and romantic experience which they recounted in after years.

The journey across Ohio and Indiana was slow because the roads were new and but little improved. The bishop and his wife often preferred to walk over the worst places. A highway had been cut across Ohio from Pittsburgh to the Indiana border at Laurel, where it was met by the Whetzel Trace. This trace was a rough sort of wagon road which had been cut through the year before by Jacob Whetzel, his son Cyrus, and four axemen. It led from Laurel to a junction with the Berry Trace near Franklin and then continued south to the falls of the Ohio.

Bishop Roberts undoubtedly came along the Whetzel Trace to its junction with the Berry Trace at what is now Franklin; but whether he could get across to what are now Spencer, Bloomington, Bedford, and Mitchell, or was obliged to turn south on the Berry Trace to the Falls of the Ohio, and thence to Mitchell over the Vincennes Trace, one does not know.

The Roberts' caravan reached their land on November 28. Lewis did not come down from Bono to meet them because he had no way of knowing when they would arrive; but the bishop knew the straggling road from Mitchell through the woods to their future home. They came out of the forest toward evening and drove down the hill to the cabin where they were to live. They were tired, and what they saw must have been depressing: only the skeleton of a log cabin—no door, no windows, no chimney, no fireplace, no floor; only log walls and a clapboard roof. Below in the flats lay a small clearing in which ripened corn was standing, but elsewhere thick woods hemmed them in on all sides.

When Elizabeth started to get supper, only potatoes were left from their provisions! Roberts took over, built a fire where the hearth was planned, and roasted the potatoes in the hot ashes. Then he laid them on a sill and said grace, as if they were sitting down to a feast. Probably he was amused as well as serious. But the child Esther, who was only fourteen and hungry, was not satisfied. She confided to the boys in a corner of the cabin, but heard by Elizabeth, that she did not "see why uncle should ask a blessing and return thanks, for a supper of nothing else in the world but roasted potatoes." [1]

The child had more to worry about when night fell upon them. Elizabeth made beds as best she could on puncheon boards which Lewis had brought up and split, but had not had time to lay. The children had but lost themselves in sleep when they were awakened by wolves howling in the woods nearby. It seemed to Esther that they would surely come in through the open door and windows and devour them. She remembered that wolves had once killed one of their horses at Shenango. Her uncle assured her that wolves were afraid of fire and that he would keep the hearth blazing all night, so she and George went back to sleep. They awakened in the morning with their fears forgotten and eager for the new adventure.

They were starting from scratch. It was as if the world they had known had vanished in the night. They had only the frame

[1] Elliott, *op. cit.*, p. 269.

of a house, their horses, a few tools, the simplest household equipment, and their strong and willing hands. About them endless woods.

"You must finish the cabin first," said Elizabeth to her husband. "Snow will fall any day now and the nights and mornings are cold. We must have a fireplace for cooking and warmth as soon as you can build one. I need a few shelves and pegs on which to hang clothing, and you must hang the kettle so I can do a washing."

Thomas called attention to the need of shelter for the horses. "We will build a shed for them after we have finished the cabin," said the bishop. "That comes first."

Breakfast over, the three men went to work on the cabin: fireplace, floor, door, windows, a half attic where the boys could sleep. It was a little cabin, about such as Thomas Lincoln built for his family in Hardin County, Kentucky. Roberts expected to build a larger one soon, but they were to live in this shelter three years before they could give attention to another. The men worked fast, and in a few days the cabin was snug for the winter. While they were building, Elizabeth cooked out-of-doors and sat on a log while she knitted and mended. What would their friends in Baltimore have thought could they have seen them?

One morning Elizabeth said to her husband privately, "Robert, we must have a cow."

"Now, Betsey," he protested, "you know we haven't enough money to buy a cow."

She persisted. "Then borrow some, or if necessary, sell one of the horses. Nothing you can do would mean more for us than to have a cow. We should then have milk for the children, and butter, cream, and milk for cooking. Surely, being a bishop, some neighbor will trust you." He yielded and managed to get the cow.

She wanted meat, and he was not slow to get it. Deer and

turkey were plentiful in the woods nearby, and he needed only a good excuse to take a day off with his rifle. His hunter's skill had not left him, and he came back with a young buck. The season being early winter, the deer was hung out-of-doors to freeze, and the family had fresh venison at will. The bishop hunted at odd times until they had enough jerked venison for the months when he should be gone. Deer pelts sold well at Bono, where there was a tannery, and with the proceeds he bought supplies and equipment for the farm. Lewis had cleared a small field and planted it with corn and potatoes in anticipation of their coming, but the yield was not sufficient for the winter.

The bishop's salary was but $200.00 and traveling expenses, and an additional allowance for the family, which he now accepted. They had accumulated savings, but these had mostly gone into the journey from Shenango and purchase of the farm. The property at Shenango had been sold for $600.00, but he realized little cash and it finally came back upon him. They could bring few things with them to Indiana and now needed everything. The proceeds from hunting, slight as they were except for meat, were greatly needed. His neighbors thought little about his hunting except to admire his skill with the rifle and to like the way he worked. They listened to him preach with greater interest, but always with a touch of deference because of his exalted position.

The big job was the clearing of land. It was imperative that they should be self-sustaining as quickly as possible and that fields should be ready for spring planting. As soon as the cabin and barn were finished, the men began on the land. They worked every moment of daylight because Roberts had to leave in March for the spring conferences, and so much had to be done before he left.

First they cleared a 10-acre field for corn, leaving the 3 acres cleared by Lewis for flax and a garden. Elizabeth wanted flax

Bishop Robert Richford Roberts—about fifty-two years of age

Monument to Bishop Robert Richford Roberts and his wife, Elizabeth Oldham Roberts, on the campus of DePauw University, Greencastle, Indiana.

for spinning and weaving. They girdled the larger trees, leaving them to be cut down later as he had done at Shenango. They cut down and burned smaller trees and grubbed out undergrowth. Esther and George, and even Elizabeth, helped the men with the brush and burning, for they were working against time. Of evenings the men built furniture from puncheon boards by candlelight—a table, stools, and one chair so heavy that Esther and George could not lift it, but had to push it over the floor. Elizabeth told these incidents to their friend, Charles Elliott, in the summer of 1843, after her husband's death.

Roberts left for the Baltimore Conference on the eighth of March. The General Conference also met that year at Baltimore on May 1. He had been gaining weight and took the strongest horse for this long ride. When he had ridden away, Elizabeth took over. The two young men plowed and dug up the fields. George was old enough to furrow a field for corn. Elizabeth, with one arm in a sling (she had an infected finger) and corn in a bag, dropped seed in the furrows, and Thomas and Robert covered them with hoes. When the bishop came back in July they had reaped a fair crop of wheat, and there was a good stand of corn. The garden also was flourishing and the field of flax, a more difficult culture, was well advanced.

They were now over the hard beginnings. Roberts negotiated for additional land while it could be bought cheaply. He used his credit to the limit. When the crops were in that fall and he had secured an abundance of meat from the forest, they were largely self-sustaining. Long afterward they looked back to this first winter in Indiana, hard as it was, with peculiar pleasure.

Chapter XV

Life at Lawrenceport

In the spring of 1820, following the first winter in Indiana, Roberts entered upon a quarter century of prodigious labor. It took him, year by year, to every part of the nation. At first he traveled on horseback, later by stage and river steamers, but always much of the time on horseback. When he took the chill which hastened his death, he had ridden home from Bedford in extreme cold on a New Year's Day.

Of the three bishops in 1820, McKendree was ailing, and the care of the churches fell largely upon George and Roberts. Of the two, Roberts was the better administrator and the more unsparing of himself. As a result, he carried the heavier burden. But the rapid growth of the church and the increasing number of conferences was soon beyond their capacity. They were reinforced by Joshua Soule and Elijah Hedding in 1824, John Emory in 1832, and Thomas Morris and Beverly Waugh in 1836.

Roberts was at home during the summer and winter months in intervals between the fall and spring conferences. He was called away, it is true, for occasional addresses, and at all times had to give attention to details of administration, but he could be with the family during these intervals and could develop his lands. Some time during these years he built a strip sawmill on the creek which flowed below the house, and from time to time bought additional farms. He not only directed the cultivation of these farms, but worked with his own hands at building, clearing fields, planting and harvesting. He also indulged his zest for hunting, and often took his rifle into the nearby woods and seldom came back without a deer or all the wild turkeys he could carry.

The family life at Lawrenceport was friendly and always interesting. In the first place, there were so many of them in the big cabin on the hill: Roberts and Elizabeth, Esther and George, his two young nephews, and relatives from Pennsylvania who came to join them. These were young and soon had friends on neighboring farms. There were marriages at which the bishop read the service. The young people would consider no other minister for this important event in their lives. Soon children were playing about and Roberts and Elizabeth were kept young in spirit.

Bishop Roberts was kindly and playful with the children. They called him "Uncle Bishop," and his wife "Aunt Betsey." They were not awed by him, but Otto Stewart, grandson of Esther and now living in Mitchell, remembers his father saying, "Uncle Bishop only spoke to us once."

The surroundings at Lawrenceport were those of a frontier society, but the home had a dignity and ease of manners which contrasted with its simplicity, and was a carry-over from their years in eastern cities. Bishop Morris, when once a guest at Lawrenceport, observed the courtesy Roberts showed to his wife. "One thing which I noticed with much pleasure," he wrote in his autobiography, "was that whoever was present to enjoy his society his wife always shared in his attentions, part of his conversation always being directed to her. He called her 'Betsey,' she called him 'Robert.' "

A portrait of Elizabeth in the historical society at Bedford reveals a face of dignity and strength, but also resignation. Hers was indeed a dedication as great as that of her husband.

Roberts wrote or sent word to her frequenly during his long

absences. "My love to Esther and the boys and, as always, to yourself," he wrote on February 8, 1822.[1] In a letter to his brother Lewis written from Tuscaloosa, Alabama, he wrote:

> Tell Betsey, my health is good, and I pray for her happiness night and day. Tell Sophia and Nancy, that I want them to take the labor of the house entirely on themselves, so that their aunt may be free from care. Tell James and George, to keep plenty of wood and meal in the house, and to do all they can to accommodate their aunt, and to make her life comfortable and happy.[2]

This is the first information that his two younger sisters had come to Lawrenceport.

They lived in the little cabin at the foot of the hill three years before they could see their way to build a larger one. They thought it more important to buy land while land was cheap—at least Roberts did. He extended his holdings slowly, 40 acres at one time, eighty at another, a quarter section at still another time. The Recorder's office at Bedford lists a total of nearly one thousand acres. He used their savings and credit to the limit to buy implements and stock these farms. He also helped his own and Elizabeth's relatives from Shenango acquire lands near them, or placed them on his own farms.

Finally they felt they could wait no longer to build a larger house. They were crowded beyond living in the cabin. Esther was now seventeen, George fifteen. James and Robert, his brother Tom's sons, were also living with them.

They selected a site on the top of the hill a hundred feet above the first cabin, and overlooking the valley of Fishing Creek. It was a much better location. The only disadvantage was the distance from the spring. They began building in 1822, but it was not completed until the winter of 1824.

[1] *Ibid.,* p. 279.
[2] *Ibid.,* p. 295.

The new cabin was built of hewed poplar logs dovetailed at the corners and reached upward the width of four logs above the first story, providing sleeping rooms on the second floor. The first floor had two large rooms eighteen feet square, with a passageway between, from which doors led into the rooms. A stairway led from the passageway to the rooms above. Each lower room had a large fireplace which opened into a huge chimney at the center of the building. Most cabins of the time had fireplaces at the ends, with chimneys built on the outside. The chimney of the Roberts' house, which was an innovation, completely closed the passageway in the middle. On the far side was a closet, with built-in shelving and doors entering the two large rooms. The first-floor rooms were plastered, using split laths. Sawed boards were used for floors, doors, and window frames. A sawmill had been built this early on one of the streams. The windows had glass panes and the roof was covered with clapboard shingles. The house when completed was a large and, of its kind, an attractive building, comfortable and convenient; and at the time one of the best in the country.

While Lawrenceport was isolated, especially when the Robertses first came to Indiana, it soon became accessible to people from a distance. By the time the new house was built, stages were passing two miles north of the farm from Bono to a junction with stages to Bedford and points north and between Louisville and Vincennes. Church officials and ministers from Illinois and Indiana were frequent visitors.

Elliott mentions one of these visits from a distance.[3] Two Indiana preachers and the Rev. G. Randall, delegate from England to the General Conference of 1828, stopped off at Lawrenceport on their way to the Illinois Conference at Madison, Indiana. The Robertses were then living in the new cabin. Randall had

[3] *Ibid.*, pp. 299-300.

formed his ideas of a bishop and a bishop's residence from what he had seen of bishops of the Church of England and bishop's palaces in the mother country.

When he came in sight of the Bishop's dwelling, he found, to his great surprise, that the American Bishop lived on a farm in a retired part of the country, and in a very common house, where there was nothing to dazzle the eye, and, moreover, where every person was at work!

Mrs. Roberts received them, told them where to feed their horses, and went to call her husband who was out somewhere on the farm. When he came in sight, one of the preachers who knew him observed that the bishop was coming. The Englishman looked out with great interest, but said he saw no bishop.

"Look in the grass lot," he was told.

He looked again as directed, but said a little impatiently, "I see a man there, but no Bishop."

"But that is certainly the bishop," said his friend.

"No! no!" he replied, "that cannot be, for the man is in his shirt sleeves."

While they were talking, Bishop Roberts entered the house, and the visitor was presented to him. He was told, to his amusement, what had been said, and they were soon in animated conversation. After a night in the Roberts' home, the visitors went on their way. The two ministers with the English delegate were Joseph Tarkington, uncle of the novelist, and James Armstrong, one of the founders of Indiana Asbury University.

For a number of years Roberts was the only bishop in Indiana, except the Catholic bishop of Vincennes. They were neighbors, living only fifty miles apart, but probably never met. Roberts soon became known over the state. He did part of his banking at Indianapolis, and after the founding of the university, was frequently at Greencastle. The photograph of Elizabeth in the historical society at Bedford, and a late one of Roberts, were taken at Kendallville. Probably he had gone there to attend a conference, and his wife had accompanied him. At Bedford he was known as a large landholder, but was also honored as their own bishop.

When Roberts came to Indiana in 1819, there was no settlement at Lawrenceport. The town was laid out and incorporated in 1837 by a group of men from Baltimore. Probably they were friends of Roberts who had known him at the Light Street Church and on one of his visits to the city had asked his advice about a location for a town. The situation on the White River seemed desirable. A big spring flowed out of a cliff on the east side where the land falls into a creek bottom, and there was a space below along the river for a boat yard, mill, tannery, distillery and warehouse which soon came into being. The owners gave the bishop two lots and named a street after him. They also built a church on adjoining lots set aside for a school. The town prospered for a time until the Baltimore and Ohio Railroad came along and by-passed it on the north.

In 1819 there was no church in the country round about. Roberts built a small log meeting house on one of his farms north of his home, where the family and neighbors worshiped until the church was built at Lawrenceport. The Presbyterians had a congregation at Bono when that town was thriving, but when the Methodists built at Lawrenceport they united with that congregation. Roberts never saw the present church but often preached in the one preceding, which burned. Lawrenceport and Bono are now ghost towns.

The last farm bought by Roberts is now owned by the Bishop Roberts' Assembly Grounds at Riverdale, adjoining Lawrenceport on the west and north. The park is used for the youth work of the Indiana Conference and is an attractive property lying along the White River. He did his last lingering work on this farm.

Sometime late in his life, just when is not known, he and Elizabeth left the big cabin with Esther and her family, and moved to a frame house on the north side of Lawrenceport. This house is standing as he left it except for a second story which was added by a subsequent owner. The large steppingstone from which he mounted his horse still stands by the side of the road, as if the beloved horseman might again mount from it some early morning to begin one of his long journeys.

Chapter XVI

Personal Traits and Incidents

IN THE EARLY YEARS OF HIS MINISTRY ROBERTS WAS TALL AND strongly built, without being heavy; but as he grew older, he gained weight. The strain upon his heart became serious many years before his death and finally hastened the end. Until three months before he died, Roberts was constantly traveling by stage, by river steamers, and on horseback, and could carry but few changes of apparel with him. He had often to tie his horse to a hitching post after a long ride and go directly into the pulpit. Gradually, with growing weariness, dress came to seem unimportant. But he was always dignified in the pulpit. When he led a hymn, when he read the Scripture, when he prayed—especially when he prayed—and when he began the sermon, people forgot his rumpled garments.

Bishop Roberts' personal trait—his generosity, kindly humor, and capricious reticence, gave rise to stories which circulated among friends and sometimes went the rounds of the church press. He enjoyed telling these experiences at dinner tables and around friendly firesides. Most of them were recorded by his friend and biographer, Charles Elliott, who often traveled with him. Some were told to him at Lawrenceport by Mrs. Roberts after her husband's death, when Elliott visited her in the summer of 1843 preparatory to writing a biography.

Roberts was generous beyond his means. Elizabeth protested, but without avail. "You will always keep us poor," she said. On the whole she was willing, for she shared his dedication of life; but her management and her toil entered importantly into the giving, and sometimes what he did was trying to her. There are records of gifts, large at the time for one of his means, to five of the colleges the church was founding. He was frequently caught by church dedications for which the bishops were in demand. He was assigned to preach and to make the appeal for money on the day of dedication. How could he press a congregation to give without personally contributing?

A striking instance occurred in New Orleans in 1825. After the close of the Mississippi Conference at Washington, near Natchez, he went down the river to New Orleans. Here the Methodists were dedicating their first church. It was a small frame building, and the congregation was poor. In the stress of the pressure for contributions Roberts sold his horse for $100.00, and gave the money to the church! He then took passage on a river steamer for Louisville, expecting to travel by stage from Louisville to Lawrenceport. Bishops were provided with travel money, either in cash or sight drafts on the Book Concern, but the horse was his own.

Bishop Thomas A. Morris describes what happened on the voyage:

On the way up the Mississippi, one very cold night, the boat struck a snag, which broke through the hull. The captain called for blankets to secure the breach; Bishop Roberts promptly flung down blanket, bed, and all, and made the best preparation he could for his own safety. The boat soon sank, but the passengers all got safe on shore. The remainder of the cold, cheerless night was spent on the uninhabited coast. Next morning, Bishop Roberts shouldered his baggage, and set off on foot up the river. After walking about seven miles, he came to a settlement, where, with the small amount of funds he had left, he bought a pony and an old Spanish saddle, and turned down the coast [the wreck was evidently above Vicksburg] so as to intersect the road from Vicksburg to Nashville. The pony being unequal to his burden, soon gave out. This was a new difficulty, as the bishop's funds were insufficient to buy another. Necessity, however, is fruitful in inventing means, and he exchanged the tired pony for a mare which had a stiff neck, and carried her head on one side near the ground, on account of which she was valued low, though a stout animal. *Old Crook-neck* carried him safely through the Indian country to Nashville, where the brethren kindly furnished him with a better horse and equipage, and likewise money to pay his expenses home.[1]

This incident brings to mind the number of times Roberts was helped by generous friends. People seemed glad to do things for him, as when he was given a suit of clothes after his sermon at the Light Street Church, Baltimore; and the next year on the Carlisle circuit, when he was given a mount after his two horses died. On another occasion, when the Mississippi Conference met at Tuscaloosa in 1828, his brethren raised a fund and presented him with a new suit of clothes. Doubtless he needed the change after the long ride from Lawrenceport.

One summer a man came sixty miles from Illinois to Lawrenceport because, he said, he "wanted to be married by a bishop." The ceremony ended, he gave the bishop a twenty-dollar gold piece. After he had gone, Roberts handed the money to Elizabeth. "Now you see, Betsey, it pays to give away money. The Lord always pays you back manyfold." She took the money with a smile, but was not convinced.

Another instance of peril by water occurred in 1828, when Bishop Roberts was traveling from Lawrenceport to Cincinnati by way of Aurora and Lawrenceburg. He spent a night with the pastor at Elizabethtown, a few miles east of Lawrenceburg and below the junction of the Whitewater with the Miami River. Both streams were in flood from the spring rains. He was persuaded to stay over the week end and to preach at a quarterly meeting.

[1] *Ibid.*, p. 301.

The regular ferry, which had to be rowed across the stream, was not running on account of the high water, but the pastor, J. H. Brower, thought he could take the bishop over since he was anxious to meet his engagement at Cincinnati. Brower wrote to his friend Calvin Ruter:

Accordingly, on Monday morning the good Bishop, with the mail-carrier, (who had been waiting for several days to get over the streams,) went to the mouth of the Whitewater, where the ferry-flat lay; and, with the two men who usually took me over, and myself as steersman, we embarked: the current was exceedingly rapid, and when about two-thirds of the distance across, (the rowers laboring with all their strength at the oars,) the lower oar suddenly snapped in twain! Thus leaving us at the mercy of the raging stream. As we were rapidly floating toward a mass of drift-wood lodged just below us, against which had we struck, we should in an instant have dashed to pieces, the only alternative was to steer the boat among a number of large trees, partly under water, and some thirty or forty feet from the shore. This we attempted; and instantly, as the gunwale of the boat struck a tree, the force of the current against the upper side pressed it down, so that the water poured over it in mass, and filled it almost in a moment. At this fearful juncture, I cried out to the Bishop to let go his horse and drive him overboard, which he did promptly, while a blow from the broken oar drove the mail-carrier's horse after him. By this expedient the load of the boat was so lightened that, by great exertion, it was pushed off from the tree, and got to the shore, full of water, and in a moment after sank. The horses made their way to the shore some two hundred yards below us uninjured, the mail bags only being lost.

During this fearful crisis the Bishop maintained a perfect calmness and self-command, to which, in a great degree, we owed our preservation. And, upon our reaching the shore, he quietly spread out his handkerchief on the wet and muddy ground, and kneeling down, several minutes elapsed before his or our own overflowing hearts . . . could give utterance to our feelings. He then broke out in the language of the 46th Psalm, "God is our refuge and strength; a very present help in trouble. Therefore will we not fear, though the earth be removed, and though the mountains be carried into the midst of the sea; though the waters thereof roar and be troubled." And then, in a strain of thanksgiving, poured out such a burst of grateful acknowledgment for, and reliance upon, the sustaining and preserving mercies of God, as befitted the solemnity of the occasion and the greatness of the escape. Then addressing me, he said, "My brother, the Lord has work for us to do yet, and has yet mercies in store for us. Let us learn never to distrust his power or willingness to preserve, and *never to shrink from the straight forward path of duty, . . .*" After accompanying the holy man to a neighboring house, where he was hospitably received, and drying his wet garments, he went on his way, and reached his appointment in season.[2]

This experience made a deep impression on his mind, a feeling of a protecting Providence and an assurance that he need not fear danger. He also had a fervent and instinctive belief in prayer, that answer came surely, and that one could expect guidance and help. In times of great stress or perplexity, as when he was debating his call to the ministry, and later when shocked by the unseemly extravagances of backwoods audiences, he went into the woods to pray and came back knowing what to do.

That he was gifted in public prayer—the most difficult kind of prayer for a sensitive mind—is mentioned repeatedly in accounts of his preaching. It is so easy for a minister to preach to the audience when he prays. Roberts seemed to talk with God and to lift the congregation with him into the divine Presence.

Reference has been made to Bishop Roberts' whimsical shyness or reticence. He always took a back seat when he entered a church where he was not known. He liked to travel in ordinary dress and to keep his identity to himself. He would slip unknown into churches where he had no engagements, and into homes where without revealing his identity he asked a stranger's lodging for the night. The habit often led to humorous and sometimes embarrassing consequences.

[2] *Ibid.*, pp. 311-12.

A story is told of a class leader who, unaware of the bishop's identity, once quizzed Roberts. The bishop had put up at a tavern. The landlord, who did not know him, was going to a class meeting and excused himself. "If you want to retire before we return," he said, handing him a candle, "you may take a bed in the adjoining room." The bishop asked if he might go along to the class meeting, if it would not be intruding.

"No intrusion at all," replied the landlord. "We allow serious persons to attend class meeting a few times without becoming members, if they wish."

The class leader, a young man with more zeal than experience, went the rounds of those present. Coming to the bishop, he inquired: "Well, stranger, have you any desire to serve the Lord and to get to heaven?"

"I have such a desire," replied the bishop.

"How long have you had this desire?"

"I cannot say precisely how long now, but for many years."

"Well, do you think, old gentleman, that you know anything about the enjoyment of experimental religion?"

"Yes, brother," answered the bishop, "I trust I do know, and have known a long time what experimental religion is; though I acknowledge I have not been as faithful as I should have been; and, consequently, have not made that progress in religion which it was my privilege to have made. Still I have a good hope in the mercy of God, through Christ, that I shall be saved in heaven at last."

The class leader gave him counsel, as was the custom, and closed the meeting, and the landlord walked back to the tavern with Roberts.

After they had been seated a short time, the landlord brought in a table, with a Bible and a hymnbook. He looked at the Bible and then at the bishop. "After a few side glances," said Roberts, "he rose, and started toward the table; then stopped, cleared his throat, and went to the door and spit; then turned again toward the table; but finally stopped, and said, 'Old gentleman, you appear to be a man who knows something of religion. It is our custom to have family worship. Perhaps you would be willing to read and pray with us?'

"I have no objection, brother, if you wish it," answered Roberts, and then proceeded to read from the Bible and to sing and pray.

"The landlord then took a candle, showed him his room; started out, got to the door, stopped, turned round, hesitated, and finally remarked: 'Old gentleman, if it would be no offense, I should like to know your name?'

"No offense at all, brother: my name is Robert R. Roberts."

When he told this anecdote, Roberts added: "And they paid me well for telling my name; for they detained me two days, and made me preach several times."

"I wished him to tell me how the young class leader looked at the close of his first sermon," said Elliott, "but he declined to make any comments." [3]

On another occasion when Bishop Roberts was traveling to meet a conference in the South, and was nearing his destination, he came to a house after dark and asked shelter for the night. It was freely given, but none of those present knew him. As dinner had been served and the dishes put away, he was not offered food. He had not had dinner, but observing that the table had been cleared, said nothing.

An attractive young minister was a guest of the family. He was the center of interest in the living room and was doing most of the talking. Roberts sat quietly in a corner for a while, listening to the conversation, but saying nothing; and finally asked to be shown to his room. An hour later the young minister was taken

[3] *Ibid.*, pp. 292-94.

to the same room. He found the stranger kneeling at the bed in prayer. When he arose, the young man found to his great embarrassment that the stranger was Bishop Roberts. Guessing that he had not had dinner, he begged to be allowed to call the family and to arrange for him to be given food, but the bishop would not consent. The family learned his identity the next morning when the two went down to breakfast. The embarrassed young minister was treated with great kindness at the conference, and in telling the incident, Roberts always refused to give the young man's name.

Much also is to be learned from portraits about Bishop Roberts' personality. If you will study the likenesses in this volume, you will observe in the first and most familiar an open, thoughtful, and kindly face. The forehead is high, the space between the eyes broad, and the brows overhanging. The face is long, the chin strong, and the lips reveal a speaking mouth. The general expression is one of thoughtfulness and power.

The second is earlier, and is more revealing. It is rugged and strong, and shows the bishop in his prime. I found a newsprint of this in the archives of the New York Conference Historical Society Library, but it was not suitable for reproduction. Finally, and most unexpectedly, I came upon the original, and a companion photograph of Mrs. Roberts, in the home of Mrs. B. F. Johnson, Orleans, Indiana. It must have been taken between 1830 and 1835, or perhaps a little later.

A third portrait is in the chapel of DePauw University. It was damaged by a fire which destroyed the old college building in 1879. A student rushed into the burning building, and not being able to drag out the full-length painting in its frame, cut out the upper part of the portrait with his pocketknife. The signature of the artist is gone, but Dr. Wilbur Peat, director of the John Herron Art Museum in Indianapolis, thinks it was done by A. A. Van Smith of Vincennes, who painted the portrait of Francis Vigo which is now at Vincennes University.

Although badly cracked, the DePauw portrait, painted the year before the bishop's death, is a vital likeness. The painting has now been restored and hangs in Meharry Hall, the old chapel of the university. The face is large and ruddy, the eyes blue, with the same half-smiling humorous look which drew people to him. The eyes are beetle browed. It is the face of a kindly man weighted with years of labor and responsibility.

Chapter XVII

Roberts' Message and Preaching

THE CHURCHES OF EVERY COMMUNION IN ROBERTS' DAY WERE fundamentalist in their thinking, as was Roberts himself. The revelations of the sciences, dealing with fossils, the formation of the earth, and the age of man came after Roberts' death. The *Origin of the Species* was published in 1859; *The Antiquity of Man* in 1863. Roberts died in 1843.

These churches believed that the earth had been created less than seven thousand years ago, instead of a time so distant that figures lose their significance. James Ussher's dates were still on the margins of their Bibles. Their concept of the inspiration of the Scriptures could not allow for errors of fact or human interpretations of the ways of God. They accepted the ancient Hebrew belief that man came from the hand of God mature and sinless, but had fallen from primal innocence by the sin of the first parents; rather than of races slowly emerging from lower forms and passing through savagery into a civilization still recent and animal in its deeper impulses. It was to them a fallen instead of an ascending race, resting under the wrath of God, unable to extricate itself, and doomed to destruction. Wesley made only one condition for those desiring admission to his societies: "A desire to flee from the wrath to come and to be saved from their sins."

Against this dark background the church lifted the tragic figure of the Son of God on the cross, a sacrifice of infinite value, satisfying divine justice and making forgiveness possible. The power this preaching gave the pioneer preachers over their audiences arose from the fact that the people held to the same opinions. They seemed not to have realized the picture this gave of their heavenly Father.

It was a simple and legalistic plan of salvation, easily memorized, and lending itself to endless elaboration; one reason why a layman with a personal experience could become an effective preacher under a system of brief pastorates. Those who have access to Adam Clark's *Preacher's Manual,* published by the Methodist Book Concern in 1826, will find this amazing Plan of Salvation set forth in the chapter entitled, "Principles of the Christian Religion." Every Methodist preacher read this little book and followed its thinking. Older persons now living will remember the ministers of their youth laboring in their sermons to explain and justify these points of view.

But the discoveries of the sciences are also a revelation of the ways of God; and, coupled with the reverent and objective study of the Bible, could have but one result. I have seen the Methodist Church, in its actual teaching, move slowly from these foundations of human thinking to the simple, axiomatic, and undoctrinal teaching of Jesus. The older theology still remains in the fundamentalist churches and in the historic statements of faith, Catholic and Protestant alike, but in the present knowledge of the universe and of history it falls strangely on the ear. The Articles of Religion of the Methodist Church are preserved in the Discipline, but children and persons seeking admission are no longer asked, "Do you believe in the Articles of Religion of the Methodist Episcopal Church?" but, "Do you receive and profess the Christian faith as contained in the New Testament of our Lord Jesus Christ?" Few persons could fathom the Articles, and certainly children could not; but to follow Christ is simpler, although the road is straight and narrow.

Roberts held to this system of doctrine and, so far as we know, did so until the end of his life. It was the common thinking of the churches, Protestant and Catholic alike. But Roberts was not a doctrinal preacher. He had seen the glory of God and had felt the love of God in his soul, and these experiences he proclaimed as living realities. He was more the poet than the theologian. His sermons were thoughtful and carefully organized, as was said by Abel Stevens. The historian of the Mississippi conferences, J. G. Jones, records that in his preaching at Natchez, Roberts spoke with feeling. Audiences were greatly moved, often to tears, and there were many conversions.

The distinctive message of pioneer Methodism was what they called "experimental religion." The term has passed out of common usage, but had positive meaning in Roberts' day. It meant that God reveals himself to the soul, and that one may know that he is a child of God. They spoke of the experience as "conversion," as "assurance," and as "consciousness of sins forgiven." In this sense it was called "experimental," after the method of the sciences. Every preacher, whatever his other qualifications, must have had this experience, or he would not be ordained. You will remember Roberts' descripiton of his own conversion in Chapter 4. The classic experience had come to him, never to be lost or doubted.

To others, perhaps to most converts in the Great Awakening, the experience came as a kind of psychic explosion. They shouted for joy. Some wept happy tears. Nature seemed changed and illumed by a heavenly light. Billy Bray said, "I can't help praising the Lord. As I go along the street, I lift up one foot, and it seems to say 'Glory'; and I lift up the other, and it seems to say 'Amen'; and so they keep up like that all the time I am walking." [1]

[1] Quoted by William James, *Varieties of Religious Experience* from W. F. Bourne, *The King's Son, a Memoir of Billy Bray.*

J. B. Finley tells of the conversion of Big-Tree, Chief of the Bear tribe on the banks of the Sandusky, Big Tree said:

> I felt so great a weight on my heart I thought it would crush me to death. I fell on my knees, and cried out, "O Father, have pity on your child that you have kept till his legs and arms are stiff with pains, and his whole body is worn out. This load will throw me down, and I shall never rise again. The trees to me will never again blossom; the corn will never again rustle in my ears, and I shall no more behold the harvest. O, take away this load from my heart, so that I can walk forth again, and see the beauty of the Great Spirit in the stars that, like watch-fires, hold their places on the borders of the hunting-grounds beyond the great river!" While I was talking to the Great Spirit, my load was gone, and I felt young again. My heart was emptied of its load, and I felt light and happy, and could run like a deer in the chase.[2]

This is what the fathers meant by experimental religion. They confidently expected the experiences of the first Christians to come to believers in their own time, and ventured everything upon the faith. They were not disappointed. They so far succeeded that they built a conquering church in the wilderness.

But, in the course of time, the preachers made a grave mistake. The scenes about their altars were so spectacular and compelling that men came to think it was the only way; and people who might have found their way to God more quietly, as did Roberts himself, and others who could never remember a time when they did not love God, were not helped and turned away discouraged or estranged. They also did not reckon with the changes that the education they were so zealously promoting would bring to people's thinking and attitudes. The time was sure to come when the public would shrink from the methods and excitement of their revivals, as Roberts himself had done in his early ministry.

[2] *Autobiography of Rev. James B. Finley* (Cincinnati: The Methodist Book Concern, 1867), p. 449.

They also carried another beautiful teaching to an extreme that finally drove it from the church. Perhaps it would be truer to say that many of them did, but Roberts was never among them. Wesley declared that the mission of Methodism was to spread scriptural holiness throughout the land. His words and the incidents which followed plunged the movement throughout England into controversy. His words became a dogma. Wesley found it necessary to warn his followers against misinterpretations and extremes, but the teaching became the doctrine of the "second blessing," and the "second rest" of Charles Wesley's hymn, "Love divine, all love excelling." Wesley wrote and rewrote his pamphlet on *Christian Perfection* in a long continued effort to clarify the teaching, and finally summed it up in one sentence: "By perfection I mean the humble, gentle, patient love of God and our neighbor, ruling our tempers, words and actions."

When so stated, who would disagree? It adds the word Godlike to the word "Christlike," as applied to human character. But the excesses of many who taught and claimed perfection were so offensive to the church and to the public mind, that the scriptural passage, "Be ye therefore perfect, even as your Father which is in heaven is perfect," ceased for a time to be the shining goal of faith and prayer.

How did Bishop Roberts preach these great messages of early Methodism? How did he appear in the pulpit? What was the quality of his preaching?

No complete sermon is left, only fragments taken down by listeners and descriptions of him in the pulpit. The most revealing of these are the sermons at Natchez in 1816 and the two sermons at Bedford and Lawrenceport three months before he died. He seemed to those who listened and knew him, to speak from a rich inner experience, and to be a prophetic voice as distinguished from a doctrinal preacher. His speaking voice was deep and resonant. He had a poet's insight and imagination, and a gift of language,

His venerable appearance in later years, his commanding presence, ease of manner and personal charm, added meaning to his words.

Two accounts of his preaching are preserved, the first by Colonel Richard Thompson who heard him at Bono, Indiana. Thompson was then a young lawyer at Bedford and was later Secretary of the Interior under President Hayes. The other is an account of a sermon by a military officer who heard him at St. Louis.

Said Colonel Thompson:

The first sermon I ever heard preached in Indiana was by Bishop Roberts, nearly forty years ago. I had just then settled in the county where he resided, and when it was announced that he would preach at Bono, near his home, I went there to hear him. I have not yet forgotten the impression under which I went. Having been raised an Episcopal, I had acquired certain ideas of a bishop which filled my mind. I had frequently heard the venerable and most excellent Bishop Mead of Virginia; and the hand of the more venerable and not less excellent Bishop White of Pennsylvania had rested on my head in the ceremony of confirmation. To these distinguished men I attached a degree of honor and respect far above that which I was in the habit of feeling for ordinary individuals. And, thus impressed, I frankly confess that I was prompted by some little curiosity to see what sort of man the Methodist Bishop of Indiana would be.

The weather was pleasant, the congregation large for the times, and the preaching out-of-doors in a beautiful grove. At the beginning of the sermon I stood at the outside of the audience, from which point for the first time, my eye rested on the venerable form of the noble old man. His gray locks were thrown back so as to expose the full view of his magnificent head and brow.

My whole attention was at once arrested, and I drank in every word as it fell from his lips, with the deepest and most intense interest, edging myself along to get nearer. His introduction was in soft but distinct tones. It was most fitly spoken in that conversational style for which he was eminently distinguished, and which is universally adopted at the commencement of his sermons. But, as he advanced, he grew and strengthened and warmed upon his subject, and displayed eloquence and power and vigor of thought. His clear and musical voice was re-echoed by the silent grove. He did not employ tropes and figures by way of ornament to the discourse—but portrayed the majesty, power and love of God in breathing words and burning thoughts that sank into the hearts and souls of his hearers. At one time, his style was simple, yet always terse, exact, and perspicuous. At others, he rose to the highest summit of eloquence. Dealing for a moment with common events, he would, without artistic action or display, carry them with him, by a sort of magic influence, into the loftier regions of thought and reason.[3]

The other occasion was told by Calvin Ruter in his funeral address at Madison, Indiana:

When attending the Missouri Conference, in St. Louis, in the fall of 1823, I became acquainted with an intelligent military officer of high rank, who, at the time, I think, had charge of a military post on the frontier, high up the Missouri River [probably Leavenworth]. . . . he inquired if Bishop Roberts would be there during the sittings of the conference; and being informed that he would not, he expressed great regret, remarking that he had heard the Bishop preach once, and would go a considerable distance to enjoy the privilege again. He added, "I was in the city when your conference held a previous session here, and learning that Bishop Roberts was to preach, I went to hear him. When I arrived, the chapel was so crowded that it was with difficulty I obtained a seat just inside the door. I saw the Bishop sitting in the pulpit; but, having been on a long frontier tour, (as I afterward learned,) his apparel looked rather rusty, and I did not suppose *that* could be he. At length he arose to begin the service. I then thought it probable that the Bishop was ill, and that this venerable looking man was put up to fill his place. I felt disappointed, but thought that I would wait a little, and hear what he had to say. He commenced reading, and I soon found I had mistaken my man. After the hymn was sung he knelt and prayed—*and such a prayer!* He read his text and commenced preaching, and I soon became so deeply interested in the speaker and his subject as to lose sight of

[3] F. C. Holliday, *Indiana Methodism* (Cincinnati: Hitchcock & Walden, 1873), pp. 326-27.

every thing else besides; and when I next came to myself, I found that I had insensibly arisen from my seat, pressed through the crowded aisle, and was standing near the pulpit, my hands uplifted, my eyes and my *mouth* open, and I was weeping *with all my might.* And O, it did me so much good to weep! I verily thought that everybody in the house was weeping too." [4]

Social Vision in Pioneer Methodism

It is often said that the churches of the pioneer period were wholly individualistic, and that the preachers were concerned only with the salvation of souls and did not have the vision of a Christian society as the end result of the Christian gospel. This is true of their emphasis. Social work, as we know it today, did not exist. The extraordinary development of welfare services in this country has come into being since the Civil War. Charity in the pioneer period was a ministry of kindness between neighbors, or of help to relatives such as Roberts gave to his nieces and nephews at Shenango and Lawrenceport. A few charitable institutions had been organized in eastern cities. The Friends had built a mental hospital and had begun prison reform at Philadelphia. Roberts knew about these institutions. It will be remembered that he was asked to speak in their behalf at public meetings in Baltimore and Philadelphia when he was pastor of the Light Street Church in Baltimore and St. George in Philadelphia.

But it would be a mistake to assume that the churches of the time lacked social vision. Pioneer society was both rough and humane. Seldom was a stranger, or a poor family seeking a home in the wilderness and asking shelter for the night, turned away from a settler's cabin. They shared what they had. Neighbor women helped their sisters at childbirth. Men plowed a sick neighbor's fields and planted a widowed mother's corn. If a cabin

[4] Elliott, pp. 313-14.

burned, people living nearby helped rebuild and refurnish the stricken household. There were no trained nurses, but willing friends brought in food and ministered to the sick. The discipline of the Methodist Church enjoined giving of alms, and class leaders were required to receive weekly contributions for the poor. Roberts' sister Elizabeth's generosity at Shenango in 1797 is a classic example of pioneer charity at its best.

Roberts himself was generous to a fault. He was always loaning or giving money to his preachers, and they were not slow to assist him. When he sold his horse at New Orleans to contribute to the erection of the first Methodist church in that city, laymen at Nashville heard about it and bought him another.

It is misleading, for other reasons, to think that the churches of the time were wholly individualistic. In the first place, the churches, then as now, were the greatest meeting places of the people on the frontier. This leisure-time function—although never thought of as such—the revivals and camp meetings, the class meetings and love feasts, the monthly visits of the preachers and their stirring sermons, the group singing, the hospitality of homes to those who came from a distance to quarterly meetings; these were bright occasions in otherwise hard and lonely lives during the frontier period.

The most pressing need of pioneer society was education for the children. Roberts realized this the more keenly because of the deprivation of his own youth. Next to the salvation of souls his greatest zeal was for education. He had not much money to give, but he had the great influence of his office, which influence he used with deliberateness and skill. His major educational interest was the founding of Indiana Asbury University at Greencastle, eighty miles north of his home. He was also interested in the seminaries the church was building in various parts of the country to bring primary and secondary educational opportunity to young people. Thirty years after his death, the church had built seventeen academies in the Northwest Indiana Conference alone.

These are all social ministries, although nobody thought of them as such. Social work, social security, public assistance, unemployment compensation, public housing, public health, community organization, social action, are recent forms of service which have arisen from the conditions of an industrial society. Their sources lie in the spirit of religion.

The great social issue of the pioneer period—and there has never been a greater—was human slavery. Wesley's first preachers sent to America brought with them the evangelical movements' opposition to slavery. One of Wesley's last letters, written on February 24, 1791, a week before his death, was sent to Wilberforce, urging him to carry on his crusade against the slave trade. Asbury was shocked at what he saw of the bondage of human beings in the land of his adoption. He confided to his Journal on January 9, 1798: "O, to be dependent on slaveholders is in part to be a slave, and I was freeborn." [5]

Bishops Asbury and Coke waited upon President Washington on May 26, 1785, bearing congratulations from the Conference and resolutions concerning slavery. They brought a petition to the Virginia legislature, which they hoped he might sign. They were received very politely and given his opinion against slavery, but Washington thought it inadvisable to sign the petition. He assured them, however, that if the matter came before the legislature, he would inform that body of his opinion. When he died fourteen years later, his will provided for the emancipation of his slaves.

The Christmas Conference of 1784, at which the Methodist Episcopal Church was organized, took extreme action. A member having slaves was required

[5] Tipple, *op. cit.*, p. 439.

to legally execute and record an instrument whereby he emancipates and sets free every slave in his possession between the ages of forty and forty-five immediately or at furthest when they arrive at the age of forty-five.

And every slave who is between the ages of twenty-five and forty immediately, or at furthest at the expiration of five years from the date of the said instrument. And every slave who is between the ages of twenty and twenty-five immediately, or at furthest when they arrive at the age of thirty. And every slave under the age of twenty, as soon as they arrive at the age of twenty-five at furthest. And every infant born in slavery after the above-mentioned rules are complied with, immediately on its birth.[6]

Those who would not comply were to be permitted to withdraw quietly or be excluded. No such persons were thereafter to be allowed to approach the Lord's Table; and no person holding slaves could be admitted to the Sacrament unless he complied. These rules were to effect members no farther than was consistent with the laws of the state in which they resided. Those in Virginia were given two years to comply. Preachers were required to keep records of masters and slaves on their circuits.

Question 43 asked: "What shall be done with those who buy or sell slaves, or give them away?"

Answer: "They are immediately to be expelled unless they buy them on purpose to free them."

The preachers found themselves immediately in an impossible situation. The rules could not be enforced. Within six months the bishops were obliged to suspend the rules, "to the deliberations of a future conference"; but added, "We do hold in deepest abhorrence the practice of slavery, and shall not cease to seek its destruction by all wise and prudent means."

The issue of slavery plagued the General Conference and the annual conferences for the next sixty years, and grew in intensity

[6] W. H. Daniels, *The Illustrated History of Methodism* (New York: Phillips & Hunt, 1887), p. 505.

with the development of the abolition movement in the North. One aspect of the situation of the churches in the South was not appreciated in the North. The southern preachers not only found public sentiment increasingly against them because of the regulations against slavery in the *Discipline,* but what distressed them most, suspicious planters were denying them access to their slaves to whom they had been preaching the gospel and whose children they had been instructing in religion. They were accustomed to criticism but this they could not endure.

Dr. William Winans of the Mississippi Conference, speaking from the floor of the General Conference in 1844, when the case of Bishop Andrew was nearing a vote, said with great feeling, "If you press this action in the mildest form in which you approach the Bishop [Andrew] you will throw every minister in the South *hors du combat;* . . . and will leave us no option—God is my witness that I speak with all sincerity of purpose toward you, but to be disconnected with your body." [7]

The debate was closed by Dr. William Capers, then Missionary Secretary, later Bishop Capers, whom the General Conference had sent to England as its fraternal delegate to the Wesleyan Conference. Said Dr. Capers:

Never, never have I suffered as in view of the evil which this measure threatens against the South. I tell you that though our hearts were to be torn from our bodies, it could avail nothing when once you have awakened the feeling that we cannot be trusted among the slaves. . . . I could wish to die sooner than live to see such a day. As sure as you live, there are tens of thousands, nay, hundreds of thousands, whose destiny may be periled by your decision on this case. When we tell you that we preach to a hundred thousand slaves in our missionary field, we only announce the beginning of our work—the beginning openings of the door of access to the most numerous masses of slaves in the South. When we add that there are two

[7] William M. Wightman, *Life of William Capers* (Nashville: Southern Methodist Publishing House, 1859), p. 402.

hundred thousand now within our reach who have no gospel unless we give it to them, it is still but the same announcement of the beginnings of the opening of that wide and effectual door, which was so long closed, and so lately has begun to be opened, for the preaching of the gospel by our ministry, to a numerous and destitute portion of the people. O close not this door! Shut us not out from this great work, to which we have been so signally called of God.[8]

Allowing for the emotional stress of debate, the sincerity and gravity of Capers' words become apparent when it is remembered that these men were opposed to slavery. They knew the condition of the slaves at firsthand. They looked upon them as children of God and immortal beings, having the same need of salvation as themselves, and destined like themselves to heaven or hell. To most of them, the Negro was a faithful friend and had been a companion in childhood. Their ignorance, their poverty, their superstition, the cruelty of some masters, and the slave's helplessness, were ever before them.

The discussion became impassioned and bitter. After a protracted debate the majority passed the fateful resolution by a vote of 110 to 68:

"*Resolved,* that it is the sense of this General Conference that he [Bishop Andrew] desist from the exercise of his office so long as this impediment remains."

The southern delegates began immediate preparations to organize a separate church for the southern conferences. They were allowed to do this without opposition, and a General Conference at Louisville the next year completed the organization of the Methodist Episcopal Church, South.

When the break came, Bishop Joshua Soule, a northern man from the state of Maine, a friend of Roberts, a companion of Asbury, and now senior bishop after the death of Roberts, cast

[8] *Ibid.*, p. 406.

his lot with the southern churches. He did so on the constitutional issue; for like all the delegates, North and South, he was opposed to slavery. The resolution, he held, violated the General Rules, which safeguarded the right of trial before a preacher could be relieved from duty, and provided that the general episcopacy should not be changed without concurrent vote of the annual conferences. Soule had drafted these rules. He became the revered senior bishop of the Methodist Episcopal Church, South.

Roberts died fourteen months before the fateful General Conference of 1844 in New York. Had he lived, and had he been strong enough to preside at its sessions, his influence would undoubtedly have been exerted to preserve the unity of the church. Had it fallen to him as presiding officer to pass upon the legality of the resolution in the case of Bishop Andrew, he would probably have sided with Soule and decided against its legality; but would he, as senior bishop, have assigned Bishop Andrew to northern conferences? I think not. The northern conferences were in rebellion against a monstrous evil. There are issues involving conscience for which at a given time no peaceable solution seems possible. As events transpired, Roberts was spared the sorrow of seeing the church he loved, and to which he had given his life, broken asunder over the issue.

Surely a church which went to such lengths and suffered so greatly on an issue of social justice, cannot be considered wanting in social awareness.

Chapter XVIII

Administration of the Conferences

ROBERTS WAS OBLIGED TO LEAVE FOR THE SPRING CONFERENCES of 1820 before things at Lawrenceport were in order, and to trust the things at home to Elizabeth. He did this of necessity, but with greatest reluctance. She had with her the two young men, his nephews, and the companionship of Esther and George, so that he need not worry about her having assistance. His brother Lewis and his family were at Bono, only four miles distant. Nor had he misgivings as to her competence, but the separation and isolation he knew would be hard for her.

The General Conference was to meet that May, 1820, in Baltimore, the first since his election four years before. He would share in presiding over its sessions with Bishops McKendree and George, and would revisit old scenes and meet old friends. They would enquire about Elizabeth and the new home in the Far West. "Why did you ever go to such an inaccessible place?" they would ask him, and he could not give them an answer that wholly satisfied his conscience.

During the next twenty-three years he was to preside over six General Conferences and to make the rounds of every annual conference at least once every four years, and many of them in intervals between. Every year would see him east of the Alleghenies. He would journey from Maine to Florida, would follow the advance of the frontier beyond the Mississippi and would observe the great valley filling with people. He would visit the areas, not as a curious traveler, but as one having authority in a vital sector of the civilization coming into being.

The hard labor of the bishops was not their travels, exhausting as they were, but their duties at the annual conferences. For six days, and sometimes as many as ten, they presided over the tedious discussions of each of the conferences. The routine was the same, following a fixed program of questions coming down from Wesley. There never has been a conference that does not have members who like to debate and who within limits must be heard. Some of them are skillful parliamentarians. The presiding bishop must watch the discussions, understand what is said, and be quick to make rulings which will stand. He must endeavor to guide discussions and save time, but he must be fair and patient. His duty is to be a presiding officer and not to enter into the discussions.

He is called upon to lead devotions, or to direct them; to ordain deacons and elders in impressive ceremonies; to preach at least two sermons, of which much is expected—one an address to candidates, the other the Sunday message; and, above all, to set the spiritual tone of the sessions. These are exacting duties which reveal the quality of the bishop's personality and his inner life.

But what tries him to the utmost is the appointment of the preachers to their churches. They are not chessmen to be moved about at will, but human beings with families. Sometimes this is forgotten. Their incomes at the time were meager, their needs great. Favoritism, or even suspicion of favoritism, was deadly. The preachers varied in ability, gifts, training, concerning which they were often unaware. Special circumstances were always arising which had to be taken into consideration.

On the other hand there were the churches, the prosperity of each of which depended on the ability of its minister. The congregations must listen to his preaching, good or bad, for at least a year. He must instruct their children, marry their sons and daughters, and bury their dead. They would be proud of him in public, or embarrassed; glad to have him in their homes as a personal friend, or hesitant to invite him. There were never enough effective men to go around.

The appeals that the bishops had to satisfy, if they could, are illustrated by letters which came to Bishop Roberts. The venerable Philip Gatch, one of the best-known and best-loved of the early preachers in Ohio, wrote to him in 1829:

> If consistent with your will and judgment, as you have George [his son] under your jurisdiction, I should be pleased if you could give him a station the coming year in one of the neighboring circuits. I am old, and the time of my departure is near at hand, and I should be glad of his company at times, while I remain in the world. He is my Benjamin; but I have freely given him up to God, and the work of the ministry. I hope you will excuse the liberty I have taken. Peace be with you.[1]

One of the preachers asked for the transfer of his brother in behalf of an aged mother, who mourned his absence; but so strong was the feeling of preachers against such transfers, that Bishops Emory and Hedding advised him first to get the approval of ten or a dozen of the leading men of the Conference.

Another request came from a distracted itinerant:

> From my family circumstances, I deem it to be my duty to make a request in reference to my appointment. My labors for the past year have been in a section of the country that is very sickly. My companion, who formerly possessed a sound constitution, has been visited with a severe attack of fever; and, before entirely recovering, she was taken with a relapse, accompanied with a state of derangement. It was thought by some that she would never regain her reason. This, however, she has regained; but not her health. There is, at present, a prospect that if proper means are used, her health also

[1] Elliott, *op. cit.*, Ch. viii; pp. 182, 185.

will be restored. Her parents live in the vicinity of this place, with whom she at present resides. I fear I could not devote my time and labors to the service of the Church, if I should have to remove my family from the care of our friends. . . . It is painful for me thus to make a request of you; as I wish to be submissive to the order of the Church in all things. I shall leave my case in your hands by barely making known my condition.

An aged minister of great worth writes:

As the interests of my motherless children require my special and personal care and attention, if you, in arranging the appointments, could indulge me in a place in one of the stations, or on the circuit of ———, it would be an accommodation for which I would be thankful. I am not wont to make such requests, and this is my first. I hope it will be excused.

On the other hand, came requests from churches for particular and desirable preachers, such as came to Asbury from the Light Street Church for Roberts. This practice was frowned upon from the earliest days because it broke the unwritten seniority rights of the preachers and limited their chances for advancement.

Bishop Roberts received an unusual request from the capital of one of the states, apparently Columbus, Ohio.

We verily believe this to be one of the most important stations within the conference. It contains about three thousand souls, is the center of the state and the seat of government. It is the residence of many public officers, is resorted to by many strangers of distinction, and has many flourishing schools, whose pupils attend the church. We want a minister whose talents would enable him to answer the expectations of those attending his ministry; to meet with promptness and counteract any improper course which our brethren of other denominations may take against us; and to secure the attendance of as many of the non-professors as possible. We have, therefore, to beg that you will send us one of your most talented preachers. Without detracting from others, we would suggest that Brother P., for many reasons, would admirably meet our wants. A sense of duty, in view of doing good, must be our apology for presenting this request. We conclude by praying that the spirit of God may preside over all your deliberations.

The request was probably granted.

Another petition, which was granted and proved fortunate, was presented to Roberts by a committee of citizens from Sandusky, Ohio, in 1828. It is highly descriptive of conditions in Ohio in the early nineteenth century. The petitioners wrote:

We have made our inquiries to such an extent as enables us to say, without hesitation, that should it be thought an object worthy your attention, and, at the same time, should it fall within the limits of your power, to send us a single man for the first year, one who is possessed of full ministerial powers and sufficient talent to attract attention, we could give him such support as would, we doubt not, yield entire satisfaction. Moreover, a fine and ample field of action would here be opened for the employment of his time and talents. . . .

We have not, as yet, any denomination sufficiently organized in our village; and, of course, we think the present opportunity highly favorable for the establishment of Methodism. Various means have been resorted to by individuals to supply this place with religious instructions; but all have hitherto seemed to be unsuccessful. The circuit preachers have visited us; though, we apprehend, to little purpose. Ministers of other denominations have, also, occasionally preached here; but our means are not equal to the high pecuniary claims of some of them. At present the popular voice seems to favor Methodism. There has been, for some years, a small society in this place, who have labored under much depression, arising from causes needless to enumerate. In order to encourage this little flock, and open a door for their enlargement, we have deemed it advisable to take our present course in petitioning you. . . . We take the liberty to make these remarks, because we are aware that a word to the wise is sufficient. Your wisdom and experience will enable you to determine whether you can meet our case or not. Please inform us of the result as soon after the close of the conference as is practicable. We would add, if we are sick we have no one to invite to console us in the capacity of a clergyman; if we are called upon in the order of Divine Providence to follow a relative or a neighbor to the tomb, we have to close the grave without religious rites; but we forbear. Very respectfully we subscribe ourselves, yours in behalf of our fellow citizens.

Who could resist such an appeal, bearing the marks of a New England town meeting? Roberts yielded and sent them the right man. The Rev. John Janes reported twenty-six new members and a successful year at the next Conference.

These difficult and sometimes heartbreaking personal problems came up for consideration at night after conference sessions while public meetings and anniversaries were going on, and these considerations were overtime work. The bishop had the assistance of his cabinet, but the final decisions were his own. How could he sleep well when the hours reached midnight? But this was not all. He must grant personal interviews to many of the preachers at odd hours to hear their special needs and desires.

Asbury was relentless about such decisions. He put the churches first—which he considered the cause of the Almighty. But Roberts was a different type of person. He, too, felt himself under Divine commission, but he was sympathetic, Bishop DuBose thought to a fault. He did his best for the preachers, as also for the churches. Doubtless, all the bishops tried to do the same, but for a man like Roberts there was an extra burden of concern.

The sessions of the annual conferences have been concentrated by long custom into the spring and fall months. They usually lasted from Wednesday until the following Monday, but have been known to continue for ten days; as, for example, the Pittsburgh Conference in 1841, over which Bishop Roberts presided. The closing session continued until ten o'clock the next Friday night. The bishop, greatly fatigued, spent much of the rest of the night going over the minutes, signing checks, and attending to other conference business which could not be delayed. He left the next morning at nine o'clock by stage for a visit to Shanango.

These annual meetings of the conferences were the hardest kind of labor for the bishops, but a grand holiday for the preachers. Usually it was their one time off during the year. They were entertained in homes of every faith in the community, and were free to bring along their wives. Food was of the best, as were the homes offered, and it was considered a privilege to entertain the preachers. The entire community was interested in the conference and thronged the public meetings. There was a fervor, a glory in singing, and an excellence in sermons and addresses; for the conference put on its best speakers, including the bishop and men from a distance.

The bishops had time for their own affairs during intervals between the fall and spring conferences, but the administration of the church constantly pressed in upon them. There were requests for addresses and dedication of churches. When a preacher died, his place had to be filled. Occasionally a preacher had to be moved and another put in his place; or, cases arose involving discipline which were always embarrassing. Correspondence was heavy, and the bishops had no secretaries.

During its first half-century the Methodist Episcopal Church also created a series of important national agencies. The Book Concern was begun in 1789 and soon assumed large proportions. The Chartered Fund, established in 1796, was devoted to the care of retired and needy preachers, and later of their wives and children. The Missionary Society was organized in 1819. Missions were begun in China, Liberia, South America, to the American Indians, and to the Negro population in the southern states. Preachers aid societies were set up in the annual conferences, beginning with the Baltimore Conference in 1827. Books, pamphlets, a theological monthly—the *Methodist Magazine,* later the *Methodist Review,* an excellent magazine—the *Ladies Repository;* and national and regional Christian Advocates, appearing weekly, were pouring forth from the Book Concern. The more important of these publications were ably edited.

While these agencies were authorized by the General Conference and had their own boards and executives, the bishops as executive officers of the General Conference were assigned general supervision and divided responsibility among themselves. Roberts assumed responsibility for missions and preachers aid. He was present at the organization of the Missionary Society, and it continued to be a major interest and an object of generous giving the rest of his life. His last great journey was beyond the Mississippi to inspect the Indian missions from Arkansas to Minnesota. Bishop Roberts was also interested in the hymnody of the church, and was himself an excellent singer. His name, as senior bishop, heads the list of six bishops who announced the publication of the Methodist Hymnbook of 1836, and signed the introductory pastoral letter to the churches. Roberts probably wrote the introductions.

Such were the responsibilities and labors of the bishops of the Methodist Episcopal Church during the pioneer period.

Chapter XIX

Zeal for Education in Pioneer Methodism

Bishop Roberts' early life was strikingly like that of Abraham Lincoln. They were both children of the wilderness. They lived fifty miles from each other in the hill country of southern Indiana from 1819 to 1829, although it is doubtful if they ever met. Lincoln had less than a year at school; Roberts the same. Their professional training, for both were members of learned professions, were much alike. Lincoln never went to a law school, nor Roberts to a theological seminary. Lincoln read *Blackstone* and the few books a frontier lawyer had to know. Roberts studied the Bible, Wesley's *Sermons,* Fletchers' *Appeal* and *Checks to Antinomianism.* Each formed his style on the classic English of the King James Version of the Bible, and his ideals on the teachings of Christ. Their memories were stored with Scripture passages which passed naturally into their speaking and writing.

The absorbing interest in education of Roberts' later years grew out of the deprivation of his youth and the shocking lack of educational opportunity which he saw about him in the Mississippi Valley. Thousands of his converts were illiterate, and their children were growing up in ignorance. As late as 1850 the census reported 75,000 people in Indiana who could neither read nor write. Roberts was great enough in himself not to feel ill at ease among educated men. This was shown by his friendship with Madison; but also, in contrast with Cartwright, he saw clearly the importance of education, and of college discipline to leaders of the people, and especially his preachers. He therefore devoted a great part of his later years and his limited personal resources to the founding of the seminaries and colleges the church was then building. He presided at one time or another over all the conferences during the early period of college building. This brought him importantly into the educational undertakings of the church.

The movement for higher education west of the Alleghenies, began around 1828-30 and was shared by other communions, especially the Presbyterians and Baptists. The Presbyterians did the early pioneering. Many of their ministers were Princeton men, or men who had studied theology there; and they had a zeal for education. They gathered the children of their neighborhoods into day schools, meeting in their own homes or in little log buildings, and taught them the rudiments of education. Doctrinal teaching was confined to Sunday sermons. They established academies in central neighborhoods, some of which later became colleges.

The multiplicity of small colleges in little towns is now considered uneconomical and not to the advantage of students because of the limited facilities they can offer students, but they were necessary and well placed in their time. Travel was difficult and expensive, and the people were poor. If their children went to school at all, it must be to nearby places. The curriculum of all colleges was limited mainly to Latin, Greek, mathematics, mental and moral philosophy, natural philosophy, and a little English and history, all taught from textbooks. Laboratory equipment was small, even in the older eastern colleges. Good teaching could therefore be done by a faculty of two or three competent teachers.

When the Methodist Episcopal Church entered the era of college building in 1828 with the founding of Augusta College, Kentucky, it was coming into its own educational heritage; for

Methodism was born and nourished in the oldest and greatest of England's universities.

As early as 1785, when poor and few in numbers, the infant church in America made a gallant attempt to build a college at Abingdon, Maryland. Dr. Coke, fresh from England and his Oxford associations, had begun at once to agitate for such an institution. Asbury supported him loyally and began to raise funds, but not without misgivings. When the cornerstone of Cokesbury College, so named in honor of Dr. Coke, was laid, Asbury preached the sermon.

The college prospered for a while. The building was one of the best in America at the time. Its situation, a few miles out from Baltimore, was admirable; but it was destroyed by fire on December 7, 1795. A second attempt was made, but the college was removed to Baltimore to a building on the grounds of the Light Street Church. This also burned, and the college was abandoned. It was believed that the fires were incendiary; but whatever the cause, the result was disheartening.

Asbury wrote in his journal on January 5, 1796:

> We have now a second and confirmed account that Cokesbury College is consumed to ashes, a sacrifice of £10,000 is about ten years. Its enemies may rejoice, and its friends need not mourn. Would any man give me £10,000 per year to do and suffer again what I have done for that house, I would not do it. The Lord called not Whitefield nor the Methodists to build colleges. I wished only for schools; Dr. Coke wanted a college. I feel distressed at the loss of the library.[1]

Asbury, though not a college man like the Wesleys, was not indifferent to education. He had received a fairly good secondary training in England and had learned Greek and Hebrew by

[1] Tipple, *op. cit.*, p. 405.

himself. He saw clearly the need of popular education and a better trained ministry. Writes Abel Stevens:

> He did not believe that collegiate or pretentious institutions of learning should be attempted by the Church while yet in its infancy, but he never abandoned the design of secondary or more practically-adapted schools. He formed, indeed, a grand scheme for the establishment of academies over the territory of the denomination, one for each "District," a District then being a Conference.

Six of these were built, but all had finally to be abandoned. The church lacked resources, and too few of its people felt the need.[2]

It is not surprising, in view of these events, that Asbury wondered whether "the Lord called not Whitefield nor the Methodists to build colleges." At any rate, the church devoted its energies for the next thirty years to evangelism. The results were phenomenal. The church grew from 287 ministers and 64,894 members in 1800 to 1,777 ministers and 476,153 members in 1830.

The church was now strong enough for its undertakings in the field of education. The Methodists, unlike the Congregationalists and Presbyterians who had long-established colleges in the East, had to build from the ground up, both East and West. They went about the task with the same energy which had characterized their evangelism. When Abel Stevens reported in 1866, the church had founded 191 institutions of learning—colleges, seminaries and theological schools. All but a very few of them were successful.

This is an extraordinary accomplishment, which the thoughtful public has not rightly evaluated. The Methodist Church has been thought of as an evangelistic movement, especially in the pioneer period, and such it was, but its concern for education was as great as its zeal for souls.

The University at Greencastle was Roberts' final and absorbing

[2] *Op. cit.*, p. 537.

concern. To this institution he gave major effort during the last ten years of his life, and he made it the residuary legatee of his estate.

The founding of the University was the work of the preachers, as of all seminaries and colleges of the early period, although the laymen came to their help when building was begun. The preachers acted as corporate groups through the conferences, and individually as pastors. Bishop Roberts was their revered and trusted leader in Indiana. He seemed, in a way, to be their own bishop since he had lived in the state since 1819. He presided over the sessions of the Indiana Conference during the organizing period of Indiana Asbury University, guided the discussions, and appointed the committees. Little will ever be known of what he did in committees and in personal interviews with ministers and laymen. Roberts probably suggested the name Indiana Asbury for the institution because he had known the great bishop so long and intimately. He always spoke of him as "Brother Asbury."

The time was indeed ripe for the undertaking. Indiana had increased in population from 24,520 in 1810 to 343,021 in 1820, and to 685,868 in 1830. There was no public-school system in the state. That was to wait another twenty years, although it had been contemplated when the constitution was written in 1816. Two small colleges offered higher education at the time: Hanover, chartered in 1827; State College, chartered in 1820 and opened in 1824. Wabash followed in 1832; Franklin in 1834; and Indiana Asbury in 1837.

By 1832 the Methodist Episcopal Church had 24,000 members in Indiana and was strong enough to carry the burden of a college. An important action by the General Conference, the separation of the Indiana churches from the Illinois Conference and their organization as the Indiana Conference, immediately preceded the movement for a college. This made the Indiana churches and their preachers an administrative unit. They could hardly have acted successfully when a part of the Illinois Conference.

The first reference to the college appears in the minutes of the initial session of the Indiana Conference which met in New Albany on October 17, 1832.[3] Doubtless, the matter had been discussed before among the preachers; for the founding of Augusta College at Augusta, Kentucky, above Cincinnati on the Ohio River, four years earlier had interested the entire church, being the first venture in the field of higher education since the burning of Cokesbury College in 1795. Bishop Roberts had presided at the Kentucky Conference during the establishment of Augusta, and came to the project of a college in Indiana with these experiences fresh in his mind.

A committee consisting of Calvin Ruter, Allen Wiley, and James Armstrong was appointed early in the session "to take into consideration the propriety of building a conference seminary." These are well-known names in early Indiana Methodism, and were to bear leading roles in the establishment of the institution.

The committee reported late in the week. The document begins with a statement of general principles. These were advanced and important points of view.

Next to the religion of the Son of God, your committee consider the light of science calculated to lessen the sum of human woe and to increase the sum of human happiness. Therefore, we are of the opinion that the means of an education ought to be placed within the reach of every community in general so that all may have an opportunity of obtaining an ordinary and necessary education. From observation and information, your committee is well convinced that where superior schools and colleges are neglected, ordinary schools are almost universally in a languished state, and many persons are

[3] The original handwritten minutes are preserved in the archives at DePauw University.

reared and live and die without any education. We therefore think that seminaries and colleges under good literary and moral regulations are of incalculable benefit to our country, and that a good Conference Seminary would be of great and growing utility to our people.

A section of the committee's report brings to light a deplorable religious controversy between the Indiana Conference and the state college at Bloomington, now long forgotten, but which at the time involved the entire commonwealth. It came within one vote of costing Indiana Asbury University its charter, at least at that session of the legislature was partly responsible for unseating a governor and his party, and held back the development of Indiana University for a generation. The issues involved seem relatively unimportant today. One wonders how good and able men could have taken them so seriously.

To understand the situation, one should know that Indiana University was begun as a state seminary by act of the legislature in 1820, and opened to students in 1824. The seminary became Indiana College in 1828 and Indiana University in 1838. It was never a Presbyterian school, but the first two teachers employed and the first president, Andrew Wylie, were Presbyterian ministers. They were chosen because of their ability, their training, and their availability, as was customary at the time. Secular as well as religious institutions turned to the clergy for teachers. But the president made the mistake of selecting all members of the faculty from the same communion.

The first historian of the University, David D. Banta, dean of the law school, who looked into the matter, could not find that the teaching staff had abused their positions by sectarian religious instruction; but that the effect was as if they had. He comments on the situation:

Right here the college management, it seems to me, was at fault. Everything should have been done that rightly could have been done to take the sting out of the charge. The Board ought to have mixed the religion of the faculty, if that was possible. The peculiar temper of the times made that a politic and a proper thing to do. The exigencies of the institution made it a proper thing to do. But the Board did nothing, and so the charge was kept up.[4]

Referring to the report of the committee to the Conference in 1832, the report recommended that the presiding elders of the five districts in the state "be required to collect all the information in their power in reference to an eligible site, and the means to build, and present the same to the next conference." Beyond this no action was taken, and final decision was not reached until the Conference met at Lafayette three years later.

The reason for the delay was that the founding of a college is a serious undertaking, involving large initial capital investment and continuing expense. Ministers never like to commit themselves to continuing appeals for money, and their feeling reflects the attitude of their congregations. Since the State College at Bloomington was a public institution, they still had hopes that they might be given representation on the faculty, and that a separate college might not be necessary. So conservative counsels prevailed, and negotiations continued.

But the administration at Bloomington, including the trustees, who were from several denominations, were inflexible. They doubtless felt that they could not yield to such pressure and that they should support their president. The Board was self-perpetuating. The Indiana Conference petitioned the legislature to make the trustees elective by the legislature, making clear at the same time why they asked for the change.

The Indiana Conference had also asked the presiding elders to circulate petitions to the legislature from over the state, which was done. The move was unfortunate and ineffective except to produce

[4] James Albert Woodburn, *History of Indiana University* (Greencastle: Indiana University Press, 1940), pp. 111-16.

violent scenes in the legislature, and to divide the people of the state on a religious issue. The feeling had not completely died out fifty years later, so persistent are religious rifts in society.[5]

There was nothing left for the church to do but to go ahead with its own college. The eventful Conference of 1835 met in Lafayette in October, Bishop Roberts in the chair. The committee on education presented a plan for setting up the college, to be known as Indiana Asbury University, but problems of faculty and curriculum were not as yet involved. The Conference decided to issue shares of one hundred dollars each, the holder to be entitled to send one student for a period of six years to the University. In a burst of enthusiasm preachers began marching up to the desk and each signing for a share. Among the names in the record is that of Bishop Roberts. This meant as much at the time as a much larger gift would mean today.

The report set an amount of ten thousand dollars as sufficient to endow a chair. This standard was followed for several years, as when money was raised for a professorship in honor of Bishop Roberts. Provision was made for gifts in lesser amounts, as low as a single dollar. Presiding elders and each preacher were made agents to raise money. To secure a site for the college, arrangements were made for competitive bids from communities to be presented to the next session of the conference in Indianapolis.

A committee of three, consisting of Allen Wiley, Calvin Ruter, and S. L. Robinson, was appointed by Bishop Roberts to draft a charter for presentation to the legislature. The committee was given power to make such adjustments during the negotiations with the legislature as should not weaken the institution. The Conference then adjourned, and the ministers went back to their

[5] For more detailed information, see: Sweet, *Indiana Asbury—DePauw University,* Ch. ii; Woodburn, *History of Indiana University, 1820-1902,* Ch. vi; Brown, *Historical Number, Bulletin of DePauw University,* pp. 4-6; *Minutes of the Indiana Conference, 1832-37.*

churches to acquaint them with what had been done and to raise money.

Meanwhile, the trustees of Indiana University, at their meeting in June, 1836, approved the appointment of Augustus Ruter, son of Calvin Ruter, chairman of the Indiana Conference committee, to the chair of political economy and modern languages. This action was at least a gesture of conciliation, but it came too late.

The committees on charter and location acted promptly and with vigor. When the Conference met at Indianapolis in October, representatives from Indianapolis, Rockville, Putnamville, Lafayette, Madison, and Greencastle appeared before the Conference. The decision went to Greencastle. The citizens of Putnam County offered a campus and thirty thousand dollars for construction of the first building. Greencastle was then a village of five hundred inhabitants, but had a reputation for healthfulness in a state plagued with malaria.

The committee appointed to draft a charter reported to the Conference at Indianapolis, and duly presented the instrument to the legislature of 1836-1837. It was granted on January 10, 1837. The charter provided for a Joint Board of Trustees and Visitors, consisting of twenty-five trustees and not to exceed nine visitors, these and their successors to be elected by the Indiana Conference and its successors. This gave control to the church, but was later modified so that the institution is a free church-related college, but not under direct church control. The present Board of Trustees and Visitors has forty-nine members: twenty-one elected in the three Indiana conferences; four by the Alumni Association; fifteen by the trustees on nomination of the president; nine visitors chosen by the conferences, but not empowered to vote.

The preamble to the charter, doubtless written by the committee of the Indiana Conference, provides that the "University is forever to be conducted on the most liberal principles, accessible to all denominations, and designed for the benefit of our citizens in general."

One is impressed by the promptness with which the corporation acted. Within two months the Joint Board met in Greencastle for organization and business. A fourteen-acre campus was secured on the southern edge of the town, and a committee made contracts for stone and bricks and the beginning of work on the college building. Progress in construction was so rapid that the cornerstone was laid on June 20, 1837. Henry B. Bascomb, President of Augusta College, one of the greatest orators of the day, gave the address.

The Joint Board arranged at the same meeting for the establishment of a preparatory school, and selected the Rev. Cyrus Nutt, a graduate of Allegheny College, as principal. When the University opened its doors in the fall of 1837, an entrance class was ready for admission. Professor Nutt was then elected to the chair of Latin and Greek in the University, and for two years was the only teacher, except for the assistance of J. W. Weakley, in the preparatory department, but he had at first only a freshman class. His was a distinguished career as teacher, minister, vice president, acting president of the college for a year following the resignation of President Curry, and President of Indiana University from 1860 to 1875.

The college-building begun in 1837 was not completed until 1842, but was enclosed and enough rooms were finished to house the school when President Simpson came to Greencastle in May, 1840. The building was of brick with limestone foundation, the stone quarried and the brick burned nearby. The total cost was $25,000. It had three stories, an attic with dormer windows, and was a large and impressive building. It provided for a chapel and classrooms on the first floor, and for classrooms, library, laboratories, and scientific collections on the second and third floors.

Bishop Roberts lived to see these events and to share in them. He saw the campus and the completed college building. He doubtless attended the inauguration of President Simpson and took part in the ceremonies. His name heads the list of the original trustees. He saw a student body of enthusiastic young men soon to become the largest in the state. His portrait in oil hung in the college chapel. When he made his will on his deathbed in March, 1843, and left the residuary of his estate to the University, he knew it was succeeding, and he could well have been satisfied. The honors which came later he could not foresee.

Chapter XX

The Last Year

BISHOP ROBERTS' LAST YEAR OF SERVICE WAS ALSO THE LAST OF his life. He died like a soldier on the battlefield. That year "he preached the Gospel," said Elliott, "in six different states, and among four distinct Indian nations in the territories west of the United States. He presided at four annual conferences; and, in the performance of his duties, traveled on horse-back, in private carriages, in steamboats and stages, five thousand four hundred and eighty-four miles." [1]

The episcopal supervision of the missions among the Indians west of the Mississippi fell to him in 1842. These missions extended from Arkansas to the headwaters of the Mississippi. Under the circumstances, considering his age, sixty-four, and his disabilities, he should not have made a personal visit to them, but should have left supervision of the missions to E. R. Ames, the Missionary Secretary, a younger man. It was characteristic of Roberts that he determined to see for himself, and nothing could deter him from the undertaking; so his last year was to begin as his life had begun, as an adventure on the frontier.

Roberts had known Indians all his life and was familiar with their tragic history. His own lands on the Shenango and in Indiana had been their hunting grounds but a half dozen years before they came into his possession. He could not fail to realize what this meant. He saw, through the massacres and terror of

[1] *Op. cit.*, p. 357.

Indian warfare, a people fighting for their homeland and using the only kind of warfare they knew. He had witnessed their exploitation and degradation, and their inability to defend themselves against a more advanced culture.

The churches had been concerned for the welfare of the Indians from the first landings in the New World, and the concern was both spiritual and temporal. Catholic priests with a zeal for souls and the martyr spirit accompanied Spanish and French explorers. Elliott and Williams in New England, the Quakers in Pennsylvania, the Moravians in Ohio, Isaac McCoy in Indiana, Alexander Talley and Capers in the South, had learned their languages, instructed their children, and taught them agriculture and the use of tools. They had done their best to protect them against exploitation and the ravages of liquor. Roberts was one of the founders of the Missionary Society in 1819, and during the first half of the nineteenth century, its major concern was the Indian.

There is an account of this visit to the Indian tribes west of the Mississippi by Ames, who accompanied Bishop Roberts on the journey. It is the more valuable because of the scarcity of detail on the life of Roberts.[2]

The rapidity of his movements is shown by this journey. He left home at Lawrenceport on January 21, 1842. He went by stage to New Albany and Louisville, where he preached four times. He went by steamer to Madison, Indiana, where he organized a new church. From Cincinnati he took stage to Lebanon, Ohio, for consultation with Bishop Soule. Returning to Louisville, he went back to Lawrenceport to see his family before the long journey to the Indian country.

On February 22 he left New Albany by river steamers to Little Rock and Forth Smith, Arkansas. He was advised by General

[2] This account of the journey to the Indian country is incorporated in Elliott, *op. cit.*, pp. 339-48. It was probably written by Ames at the request of Elliott.

Taylor of the U. S. Army not to visit the Choctaw country. On March 15 he started north by buckboard with Dr. Ames through the Cherokee, Seneca, and Shawnee reservations.

He spent two weeks with the Cherokees. One of the Indians, on seeing him inquired who he was. On being told that he was the grandfather of all the missionaries, said, "Well, he look it."

The journey led over the prairies of Arkansas and Missouri during the period of spring freshets and wild storms. On April 11 they made forty-five miles over a treeless prairie, most of the way in a violent storm. Every little stream became a torrent. Ames writes:

In the midst of the storm, we arrived at the bank of a considerable stream, called the Dry Wood, which was any thing but dry wood then. It was rising rapidly, and appeared as if it would soon be swimming deep, if it was not so already. The banks were at least forty feet high, and steeper than the roof of a house. What was to be done? It was impossible to stay where we were, and it seemed equally so to go forward; but it was determined to make the effort. I handed the lines to the Bishop, took the near-horse by the bit, and led them to the bank of the stream. The horses planted their feet, and down we all slid together; but it was impossible to stop at the water's edge; and before we could call a halt, I was waist deep in water. But the stream was finally passed in safety; and after losing our way, and traveling three or four miles through the rain, another similar stream was crossed by a similar process; and shortly after, weary, wet and hungry, the place of destination was reached.

At the falls of the Marie des Cygnes, where they hoped to spend a night, the French trader would not give them shelter.

He seemed quite grim and said he was not prepared to keep travelers. I assured him that we were not at all particular about our personal accommodation; if we but had a fire and shelter, we would be satisfied; our principal anxiety was to procure some grain for our wearied horses. He replied that he had no grain except what he bought, and that we could not stay. While this colloquy was going on, the Bishop sat in silence on the hind-seat of the carriage; and as the curtains were down, and it was getting dark, the trader could not see him. All the French traders in the Indian country are Catholics, and it just then occurred to me that we were not more than eighteen or twenty miles from a Catholic mission among the Pottawatomies. So I thought I would try an experiment. And, turning round on my seat, I said, with great deference, but quite audibly, "*Bishop,* what is to be done?" "Why, we must get some fire and camp out," he replied. No sooner did the sound of the title fall on the Frechman's ears, than an entire change was at once produced; and hearing the Bishop's reply to my question, he exclaimed, "O, by no means, gentlemen: you shall be very welcome to stay." And stay we did; and both ourselves and horses fared exceedingly well. And the Bishop's title, which I did not fail to use on all occasions, after I discovered its value, paid all expenses.

On April 14, as the party was lunching beside a big spring, and Bishop Roberts was saying grace, the horses broke loose.

In three minutes, they dashed, at the top of their speed through the brush, down into a hollow: there they upset the carriage, crushed the top all to pieces, broke the tongue, and one of the whipple-trees and tore loose the other: then away they went over an eminence, where they were out of sight. The carriage was turned right side up, and after tracing the horses two miles they were found quietly feeding in a little valley, and were brought back. By this time, it was probably four o'clock. One of two things had to be done: we were either to mount the horses and ride to the mission, which was thirty or forty miles distant, and there get someone to come back with a team, and after taking the carriage apart and putting it into a big wagon, bring it to us, or by some means it was to be patched up so that we could travel in it. It was finally determined to try to repair the carriage, and camp there all night. Before leaving Louisville, I remembered that a carriage might be upset and broken in an Indian country where no mechanics could be met with, and I, therefore, prepared myself with some gimblets, nails, screws, and a hand axe, etc. They were accordingly used, and to such good advantage, that by eight o'clock next morning the carriage and harness were as strong, if not quite so neat, as they were before. The night, however, was not passed without considerable discomfort to the Bishop.

April 15. After traveling hard all day, without even stopping to eat a mouthful of food, we reached the Indian Manual Labor School about dark. Thus did the old man, bending under the weight of more than threescore years, travel two days without food, except a small quantity of cold meat and bread, and pass the night without a tent, or even a blanket to cover him. . . .

The Bishop had promised himself great satisfaction from his visit to these missions; but was much cast down by learning on his arrival that the Rev. William Johnson, the superintendent, had *died* the week before. He had been laboring among the Indians for ten years, and was universally beloved and confided in by them. The arrival of the Bishop was most opportune, as it was requisite for him to appoint another superintendent, and make some other changes which the death of brother Johnson had rendered necessary. After spending a day or two in examining the condition of the school, farm, stock, mechanics' shops, etc., and offering some suggestions as to the best mode of conducting the establishment, and making some slight alterations, he proceeded to visit the missions, and preached among the Shawnees, Delawares and Kickapoos. He enjoyed himself very much, and was greatly pleased with the condition of the missions; and also with what he saw on his visit to the Moravian mission among the Delawares, and the Friends' school among the Shawnees.

Having disposed of the carriage and horses on the 4th of May, the Bishop took passage at the Kansas landing [3] on the Missouri River, for St. Louis on the steamboat, *Oceana*, and arrived at his destination on the 7th. He preached in the city twice, and assisted at the laying of the corner stone of the Centenary Church. He concluded to relinquish his intended trip to the missions on the Upper Mississippi; and on the 10th of May, started for home by way of Louisville, arriving about the 20th.[4]

After returning from his long journey from the Indian country, the bishop remained at Lawrenceport for the next five weeks.

[3] This was later Independence, the beginning and outfitting point for the Santa Fe and Oregon Trails.

[4] Elliott, *op. cit.*, pp. 345 ff.

In a way he rested. To be with Elizabeth in the quiet of the hills, surrounded by George and Esther and their children, was grateful to his tortured body. He rode over the farms and did a little work with his hands, but only a little, for he tired quickly. Elizabeth watched over him anxiously and did what she could. The two households were gentle and solicitous for his welfare. He went to the little church in the village and preached to his neighbors on one of the Sundays. He said grace at meals as if the Master were an unseen guest, and gathered the household together for Scripture and prayer.

On the twentieth of May a letter came from President Simpson and E. R. Ames, reminding him that the Indiana Conference had asked that he allow his portrait to be painted, and requesting him to stop off at Greencastle for sittings on his way to the Rock River Conference, which was to convene in Chicago on August 3. "We need scarcely remind you," the letter read, "that your advanced age and arduous labors admonish us to secure, while we may, an accurate likeness of one who has been identified with so much that deeply concerns our Church, and who, to so many of this conference in particular, has been a spiritual father and guide." They would send a carriage for him in due time, the letter continued, unless he should write that he could not come.[5]

The Rev. Isaac Crawford of the Indiana Conference came to Lawrenceport the last week in June and drove the bishop to Greencastle. Here he remained two weeks, the guest of the college, while the portrait was being painted. The portrait was hung in the chapel in a place of honor.

The bishop had a pleasant two weeks at Greencastle, and it was while he was sitting for the portrait that President Simpson took down in longhand from the bishop's dictation the account of his life.

[5] *Ibid.*, pp. 349-50.

From Greencastle Roberts was driven by Crawford to Chicago. He stopped on the way to see his brother Lewis at Ashgrove, Illinois, near Watseka, and arrived in Chicago in time for the Rock River Conference on August 3. He preached on Sunday and ordained elders and deacons. On Monday night he attended the anniversary of the Missionary Society, which he seldom missed.

On the twelfth he left for the Illinois Conference at Winchester. This was a large and fatiguing session, and it was evident that he was greatly exhausted, but he held up and neglected nothing. From Winchester he was driven in an open buggy three hundred miles in sweltering August heat to Jefferson City, Missouri, the seat of the Missouri Conference. How he endured the drive and held up during the Conference is a wonder. He said frequently to Ames, who was with him, "I am doing my last year's work."

This was the twenty-eighth session of the Missouri Conference. Roberts had presided over fourteen of the twenty-eight. He seemed to belong to them, and was loved and venerated as their father in God. After the Conference had finished, except for the reading of the appointments, church people and citizens met with the preachers in the courthouse for the final session. The bishop, leaning on his cane, arose to speak. He reminisced about the growth of the church in his lifetime. He recalled his presence at the first meeting of the Conference, rejoiced in its growth, and mentioned names of men familiar to them, some of them dead, some in his presence. "My age and increasing infirmities admonish me," he said, "that my work is nearly finished. I expect never to see you again. Walk in the old paths. Follow the Great Shepherd, and all will be well. I feel like a father leaving his children. God be with you. Goodbye." Preachers and people were not ashamed of tears.

Leaving Jefferson City, the bishop took another long drive, halfway across Missouri, entirely across Illinois, and sixty miles into Indiana to his home. September on those plains of great rivers is hotter than in the South, but he lived to reach Lawrenceport. Even more, he rallied, and a few weeks later went to the Arkansas Conference at Helena; but he was feeble. Fortunately Bishop Andrew was present and took the heavy burden from his shoulders. This was Bishop Roberts' last conference.

Chapter XXI

The End of the Road

WHEN ROBERTS CAME BACK FROM THE CONFERENCE AT HELENA he was dragging his feet; but under the influence of sun and air and the quiet life at home, his strength began to revive. The family was now living in a pleasant frame cottage on the north side of Lawrenceport overlooking the valley of the White River. It was on the farm which is now the Bishop Roberts' Assembly Grounds of the Indiana Conference at Riverdale, where the youth societies of the conference meet every summer for instruction and recreation. Esther Stewart and her family were living in the big cabin at the homeplace.

The bishop was soon mounting his horse from the steppingstone in front of the house (it is still there) and riding over his farms. He even ventured out to where men were clearing land and took a hand at burning brush. He was not strong enough to use an axe, but it seemed as if his strength were returning and that he might resume his work.

Suddenly, on the twenty-seventh of December came a devastating blow. His nephew George Roberts died unexpectedly after a short illness. They had taken him into their home when a child of six and loved him as if he were their own son. George had married a daughter of one of the preachers and had a family of small children. The bishop had arranged that George and his family should come to the house, and that he and Elizabeth should live with them. Now he was dead at thirty-six.

On the eighth of January Roberts wrote to his brother Lewis in Illinois:

> The affliction in our family circle during the last year has been very great. The room in which George breathed his last, is the one in which his son Thomas died, and, also, Susan Oldham, a few months before him. . . . You will learn from this intelligence that my plan of boarding my family with George is set aside. But the rest of us live together yet, and probably shall continue to do so until spring; and it is possible that then I shall move to the old place, as Betsey now seems willing, or more than willing, to go. But all these things are concealed in futurity; and I pray to be resigned to the will of the Lord both in life and in death.[1]

The winter of 1842-43 set in early and continued with unusual severity. The cold and the icy winds affected Roberts' throat. He had been afflicted with asthma for many years. He found himself less able to resist these recurring attacks, but he would not allow them to interfere with his work.

Four days after George's death he left the stricken family at Lawrenceport to keep an engagement at Bedford, ten miles distant. He had promised the pastor of the church to open a revival meeting with a watch-night service, and to preach the sermon on New Year's Sunday morning. He took the river road and went on horseback. This was on Saturday morning. That night he shared in the watch-night meeting and closed the service at midnight. He spoke of the brevity and uncertainty of life, reflecting his own mood of recent sorrow and physical weakness, and urged his hearers to make the most of their remaining days. Then he prayed, and rising from his knees, led them in singing.

On Sunday morning the bishop preached what his friend and lawyer, John McDonald of Bedford, called an inspired sermon. He chose a text from Proverbs: "He that loveth pureness of heart, for the grace of his lips the king shall be his friend." He

[1] *Ibid.*, pp 366-68.

poured into the message the experience and passion of his ministry; the power of love to make a human life beautiful and strong; the glory that touches even the lips with grace; the pure in heart who see God.

When he spoke of the "friendship of the king," he became eloquent. He told them he knew he had not long to live. "My work is almost done. These trembling hands, these whitened locks, portend the end. But it matters little, for I have not words to describe what lies ahead of me in that land where the King shall be my friend." The sermon was followed by the celebration of the Lord's Supper, but he was too exhausted to assist, except at the consecration of the bread and wine.

The following day he rode alone back to Lawrenceport. His friends urged him to delay until the weather was more favorable, but he had bought books for a school which was to begin in Lawrenceport that day, and he felt that he must not disappoint the teacher and the children. The weather was extremely cold, and although he was warmly clad, he became chilled through and through and took a violent cold. His asthma came back with a vengeance. When he reached home, he was so ill that Elizabeth urged that they send for a doctor; but her husband was unwilling to ask him to come through the snow and cold, so they resorted to household remedies.

He rallied from this attack, and by Sunday was able to go to the village church. The building was but a block and a half away. There had been a heavy snow the latter part of the week, and the preacher in charge was not able to get through the drifts to Lawrenceport. After waiting a while with the congregation, Bishop Roberts ascended the pulpit and took the service. He led the singing of Charles Wesley's hymn:

O for a heart to praise my God,
A heart from sin set free.

After this he prayed. When he arose to preach, he read the sixth Beatitude. "Blessed are the pure in heart, for they shall see God." It was the same theme he had used at Bedford the Sunday previous, but he had taken a different text.

This was the last sermon he ever preached. How significant that he chose the same theme for his last two messages. It was not the usual sermon on holiness—the hard, critical, doctrinal sermon—but as if he spoke from the fullness of heavenly love abiding in his own heart.

Elizabeth had written Lewis in Illinois to let him know of the increasing seriousness of his brother's condition, and on the ninth of February Lewis arrived in Lawrenceport. There seemed no immediate danger, and friends who came to the house were allowed to see the bishop. But toward the end of the month he grew rapidly worse, and Dr. Cavin from the nearby town of Springfield was called in. After Dr. Cavin's visit and under his treatment he was better for a time and was able to receive friends, although he could converse but little. Edward R. Ames, the missionary seceretary, came from Cincinnati to confer with him about the Indian missions.

Ames reported that the bishop seemed better, but was very feeble and unable to converse except with strain.

> As I was obliged to leave in the morning, I said to him that there were some matters which I wished to communicate to him, but I feared it would weary him. He replied, "No, I am glad to hear you talk, but I cannot say much myself." After listening to the facts which I had to communicate respecting some of the subjects which would come before his colleagues at their approaching meeting, he gave his opinion in a few words, and desired me to request Bishop Soule to act for him in things pertaining to the missions. This, I presume, was the last official act of his life.

He was so much worse after Ames' visit that on the fourteenth of March he asked to see his brother Lewis and his friend and lawyer, John McDonald of Bedford, to help him arrange his affairs and make his will. This was done, and after it had been read to him, he raised himself in the bed and signed the document in the presence of witnesses. The transaction was an ordeal and required great effort.

His friend, the Rev. W. Terrell, came to see him, and at a time when he appeared to be at ease, asked him if he still felt the same confidence he had expressed to him on his former visit? The bishop replied that he did, and then added, "Brother, I feel that if I die I shall die in the Lord, and if I live I shall live in the Lord." "In neither of the conversations I had with the bishop," said Terrell, "did he evince anything like ecstasy. Indeed, I thought he appeared to be tired."

The sick man lay on a bed in a pleasant room on the left of the entrance hall. A fire was kept burning in the fireplace, for it was still winter. The household moved about quietly, ministering to his needs while the days dragged by. It must have seemed to him at times that he could not live and that he could not die. Elizabeth went about the house saying little, but was with him day and night. Hers was the deeper sorrow among the watchers. George had gone, and now her husband was leaving her, not to return again as he had done so often from one of his long journeys. Her life's house of dreams was falling about her, and she was silent with grief. She remembered the time when he had told her, in response to her anxiety that he might die when away from home, as he came so near doing at Port Gibson on his way back from Natchez in 1816, that he had received an assurance that he would die at home. When she asked him how the assurance came, he told her that it was while engaged in prayer. Now it was coming true. He was dying at home, and in her presence.

The church at large and friends in distant places were wholly unaware of what was taking place at Lawrenceport. They did not know until the news reached them and all was over. Roberts died at one o'clock on the night of March 26, 1843. He was conscious at the last and apparently died without pain. He looked around upon them all, lifted his hands as if in blessing, and fell back into unconsciousness.

The next morning neighbors carried the news through the countryside. Couriers were sent to Bono, Mitchell, and Bedford. It was impossible to get word to friends at a greater distance. It was decided to bury him on the old farm, in a cornfield in front of the cabin. The decision was probably made by Elizabeth. She wanted him near the house where they had lived so many years and where she expected to spend her remaining days.

Such burials were frequent in pioneer times when as yet there were few common cemeteries. The traveler comes upon these little plots of burying ground here and there on the older farms, most of them neglected after the passing of years. The headstones show white among the briars, and the enclosing fence has fallen down. A time comes when the graves are moved, or plowed under by unknowing hands, and the place that knew them knows them no more.

The funeral service was held in the home at Lawrenceport on Tuesday morning following his death on Sunday. When Roberts bought the house, he had removed a partition between a front room and the kitchen to make one large living room where neighborhood meetings could be held. This room also had a fireplace. Here the Rev. E. G. Wood conducted the service and preached the funeral sermon. They had expected to proceed immediately after the service to the grave, but the weather was so violent that it was necessary to defer the burial until the next day. He seemed fated to make so many of his hard journeys in winter. The farm lay two miles south of the village. His friend, Charles Elliott, visited the place the summer after the bishop's death and wrote about it with grief and pain:

This spot is in a remote corner of Lawrence county in a secluded neighborhood—to or near which no leading road conducts the traveler. Either horse-paths or scarcely visible wagon-tracks, lead to the farm. With the best directions, it would be difficult for a stranger to find the place where he was buried. In this sequestered spot, for several months, laid the remains of the senior Bishop of the Methodist Episcopal Church, who had been forty-one years a traveling preacher and twenty-seven a Bishop, and who, in performing the arduous duties of his charge, had traveled in twenty states of the Union during one year.[2]

Only his dedicated and resolute will had carried him through; but now he had come to the end of the road. His work was done. He had been faithful to the last. His grave in a cornfield, cleared from the primeval forest by his own hands and in such a remote and silent place, is spectaular in its symbolism of the bishop's life. But a lonelier grave could not be imagined, unless a burial at sea.

When the news of Roberts' death reached the churches, there was a shocked reaction of surprise and grief. It was known that he had visited the Indian missions and that he had met the conferences in Illinois, Missouri, and Arkansas; and it was expected that he would attend the General Conference of 1844 in New York. The church press had kept the membership informed of his movements, but now he was dead and vanished before his friends knew of his illness.

The events which followed when the news reached the church reveal the regard in which he was held. Memorial services were held at the General Conference and by the annual conferences throughout the connection. There were special meetings in Cincinnati, Louisville, Madison, Indiana, and Dayton, Ohio, to mention a few. Dr. James B. Finley preached the sermon at Dayton, and Dr. Henry B. Bascom at Louisville. His friend and

[2] *Ibid.*, pp. 381-82.

biographer, Charles Elliott, editor of the *Western Christian Advocate,* spoke at Cincinnati.

A spontaneous feeling arose among the churches that his body should not be left in its remote grave. Friends in Baltimore requested that he be brought to that city and laid beside Asbury and Emory beneath the pulpit of the Eutaw Street Church. Louisville, Madison, and Cincinnati desired to have him there. The decision was finally made by the Indiana Conference, for he rightfully belonged to Indiana. This Conference, which then included the entire state, met in Crawfordsville on October 18, 1843, five months after the bishop's death. Amidst deep feeling, formal resolutions were passed expressing the affection of the ministers for their chief pastor, and asking for the removal of his body to the campus at Greencastle.

Carrying into effect these resolutions, a committee of seven ministers drove to Lawrenceport in January, 1844. The original plain handmade casket was placed in another of two-inch oak planks and brought the eigthy-five miles to Greencastle. In the meantime, the trustees of the University met and authorized interment on the campus. The committee bringing the body, accompanied by the family and friends from Lawrenceport, were met at the city limits by a procession of ministers, faculty, students, and citizens, which then moved slowly through the streets to the college chapel. Here the bishop lay in state under an honor guard of ministers until next morning.

The address was made by Professor William Clark Larrabee of the University faculty, himself a minister, writer, and personal friend of Bishop Roberts. He recounted the events which led to the reinterment on the campus, and pointed out the appropriateness of his resting place:

> To us it appears, that no place so suitable as this could have been selected. Though Bishop Roberts was deeply interested in the prosperity of the church in every section of her widely extended

work, yet among all her literary and benevolent institutions this university was his favorite. He made the Indiana Asbury University his only residuary legatee, bestowing upon it all his property which could be spared after supporting his aged widow and assisting some dependent relatives.

Dwelling upon the passing of cities and the decay of burial places, he contrasted the permanence of a university.

A lonely woman listened to Professor Larrabee's address in the chapel and stood beside the grave that winter's day. It was Elizabeth Oldham Roberts, the bishop's wife, the bride of his youth and the love of his life. They had lived together forty-five years since their honeymoon in the forests of western Pennsylvania in the late winter of 1798. She had shared the hardships, and, to an extent, the excitement of his life.

Roberts had always been anxious about Elizabeth. She had been so much alone, while his life was so full of adventure. He knew how much she had enjoyed their eight years in eastern cities, and how hard it had been for her to bury herself in the backwoods of Lawrenceport. He also knew how loyal and competent she had been. Her only portrait, taken late in life, reveals both strength and resignation. When he faced the imminence of death, his great concern was for her. He consigned her to the care of Esther, gave Esther the home farm for the purpose, and left another farm at Elizabeth's disposal. He knew also that she should receive annual grants from the conferences; but he realized that nobody could take his place, and he feared what advancing years might bring to her.

Hers indeed had been the more difficult lot. He had had the advantages of travel, of wide associations with interesting people, and of constant speaking. His mind had been developed by responsibility. The intellectual ferment of the time had stimulated his thinking. Since they had left Philadelphia in 1816, she had lived mostly in isolation, in inaccessible places, with only the children and a few pioneer families as neighbors. Only occasionally did she get away and then only for short periods. During the first hard years she worked with her hands, like the pioneer women about her. He did the same, but for him physical labor was a welcome change from travel and speaking.

But for his love and thoughtfulness he would have grown away from her, but he never did. He wrote to her constantly on his journeys and kept her in touch with his thinking and doings. They had many visitors at Lawrenceport from the larger world in whose friendship and conversation she shared. She had learned the ways of eastern cities when they were at Baltimore, Alexandria, Washington, and Philadelphia. People remembered her with affection. When he was at home between episcopal journeys, sometimes two and three months at a time, they were constantly together.

When he died, her life was completely disrupted. She went to live with Esther at the old farm and found herself no longer mistress of a home. She was comforted by the nearness of her husband's grave, which she could see from the window of her room, but when his body was removed to Greencastle, her loneliness became intolerable.

Some time after her husband's death—when, nobody living knows and no record remains—she left the home with Esther and moved to Greencastle. One can only surmise why she left. It is always difficult for a woman who has been mistress of her own home for a lifetime to be a passive guest in her former home. Doubtless, also Elizabeth was attracted to friends and the more interesting life at Greencastle. But the compelling reason was emotional. She wanted to be near her husband in the place where he was so greatly honored and remembered. She had sufficient income from the farms and the annual grants from the conferences to meet her needs.[3]

[3] The grants are listed in the Minutes of the conferences, year by year,

No arrangement could have been more fortunate for her, or more pleasing to her husband, could he have known. The house was a block west of the campus and two blocks from Roberts' grave. The people of the church and the university were kind to her and treated her with distinction. She passed by the grave on her way to church, and whenever the mood impelled her, and she was measurably happy.

Elizabeth lived fifteen years after her husband's death—eight years at least in Greencastle. That Elizabeth Oldham had the care her husband so greatly desired is certain.

She died on December 17, 1858, at the age of eighty-two. Loving hands carried her to the campus and laid her beside her husband. They were together again in physical nearness, if insensate, and there they lie today. They died in the hope of eternal life and in the expectancy of a reunion in which they fervently believed. When a marble shaft was erected over their graves the year after she died, under her name was inscribed the simple epitaph: "She worked willingly with her hands." It was written by Bishop Soule. There could have been no more fitting or eleoquent summary of her life.

Thus came to an end the lives of these two unselfish and courageous persons. No one is now living who knew them. Their names are passing into legend in Indiana. The cabin on the farm at Lawrenceport has been dismantled, and only a pile of rocks from the huge fireplace marks the spot. The marble shaft on the campus stands as it was, except for the weathering of many winters. The graves have never been moved, nor are they likely to be. They lie in the open quadrangle between Asbury and John H. Harrison halls, and are faced by the new Roy O. West Library, which stands on the site of the original college building. Every

designated to "Mrs. Roberts," or "Widow Roberts." They were never large from any one conference; but there were many conferences, and the purchasing power of money was much greater than today.

year on Founders' Day an academic procession moves from the chapel to the monument, and a wreath is laid on the grave. When the college opens in the fall, and newly arrived students are taken in groups and shown about the campus, they pause at the monument and are told the romantic story of those who lie beneath.

If the Methodist Church canonized its most saintly leaders, Bishop Roberts might well be named the patron saint of the University.

It is futile to attempt to estimate the greatness of a man relative to his contemporaries. Certainly, it would have been abhorrent to Roberts himself. This much, however, can be said with restraint: He was an excellent administrator during the formative period of the church and its phenomenal development in the Mississippi Valley. He was singularly prepared for his responsibilities and showed great wisdom and devotion in their execution. He relied upon fairness and choice of men for his preachers and gave them freedom for the use of their abilities. He wanted to help them as well as to advance the church to which he had given his life; and he always thought last about himself.

He was equally successful as an evangelist; that is, in persuading men to follow Christ, and in helping them achieve in their own hearts the joyful experience of communion with God. This great gift of Bishop Roberts has not been sufficiently recognized in references to his preaching and personal ministry. He used none of the spectacular methods of Lorenzo Dow, nor the high-pressure evangelism of the present day, but won men's hearts by his sincerity and his manifest knowledge of spiritual reality.

He had a zeal for education as great as his passion for souls. This concern he shared with the church. Nothing more definitely reveals the breadth and clarity of his mind. The campus on which he was buried was his supreme educational interest; but he was equally involved in the extraordinary accomplishments of the church in the fields of primary and secondary education.

His greatest influence lay in his character. There is universal testimony by his contemporaries to the saintliness of the man himself. I have not come upon the slightest evidence of the ordinary weaknesses that lead men astray, nor of the subtler form of pride and vanity of which good men seem so often unaware. His faults—if they can be considered faults—were his extreme reticence, bordering upon eccentricity; his passionate love of the soil, and his love of hunting. Perhaps these rather serve to endear him to us, as do some of the common ways of the saints. I am disturbed only by the excess of the devotion which led him to subject Elizabeth, his wife, to the hardships of the early days at Lawrenceport. I have often thought about her and what she endured; but always remember that they were pioneers, to whom such experiences were not unusual; that the women about her had less to inspire them, and that she shared with her husband in a common dedication of life. As Bishop Soule wrote so understandingly in her epitaph: "She worked willingly with her hands."

The most discerning estimate of the life and work of Bishop Roberts is that written by Bishop Joshua Soule at the request of the Indiana Conference for the monument on the campus at DePauw University:

SACRED

TO THE MEMORY OF THE

REV. ROBERT R. ROBERTS

Bishop of the Methodist Episcopal Church in the United States of America:

Born in Frederick county, Maryland, August 2, 1778;
And died in Lawrence county, Indiana, March 26, 1843.

He was elected to the Episcopal office in May, 1816; which holy
Vocation he sustained, unblamably, to the close of his life.
In this devoted servant of Christ were united, in an eminent degree,
The Scriptural qualifications of an Apostolic Bishop: sound in
The doctrines of Holy Scripture; deep in the experience
Of the grace of God; firm, yet gentle and conciliating
In the discharge of his official duties; apt to teach;
Patient in tribulation; abundant in labors;
Fervent in spirit; given to hospitality.
He preached the Gospel of Christ, as an itinerant, with great success,
For more than forty years, embracing a period of
Extraordinary increase and prosperity in the Church,
To which his labors greatly contributed.
For almost twenty-seven years, he performed the arduous duties of
A General Superintendent, traveling constantly through the
United States and Territories, with that self-sacrificing
Devotion to the interests of the Church, which is
Worthy of a true successor of the Apostles.
He possessed a strong understanding and sound judgment.
In all the labors, sufferings, and perils of his long and eventful life, he
Manifested that evenness and unshaken fortitude of mind
Which are essential elements of real greatness.
His preaching was in the demonstration of the Spirit, and of power;
And in the final reckoning, it will appear that many
Were turned to righteousness by his ministry.
In his life and labors, he has left an illustrious example to those who
Survive him, and a sweet savor which will embalm him in
The memory of the ministers and people of his charge.
He rests from his labors, and his works follow him.

Bibliography

Sources

The chief sources on the life of Bishop Roberts are the three biographies and the Simpson manuscript mentioned in the Preface. *The Life of Robert R. Roberts,* written in 1856 by Benjamin St. James Fry for the young people of the church, is adapted from Elliott. William Clark Larrabee's life of Roberts is one of a series in *Asbury and His Coadjutors.* Larrabee knew Roberts personally. The source for all subsequent writers is the Elliott biography. In addition to these major sources, there are widely scattered materials from which the bibliography is selected. Much information, which appears in the text, has rewarded field research.

Official Publications

Minutes of the Conferences
Minutes of the General Conferences—1784-1844
Minutes of the Indiana Conference—1832-44
DePauw University Archives
Disciplines of the Methodist Episcopal Church

General

Buckley, James M. *History of Methodism.* 2 vols. New York: Harper & Bros., 1897-98.

Crooks, George R. *The Life of Bishop Simpson.* New York: Harper & Bros., 1890.

Daniels, William H. *The Illustrated History of Methodism.* New York: Phillips & Hunt, 1887.

Du Bose, Horace W. *The Life of Joshua Soule.* Nashville and Dallas: Publishing House of the Methodist Episcopal Church, South, 1916.

Henkle, M. M. *The Life of Henry Bidleman Bascom.* Louisville: Morton & Griswold, 1854.

Hoss, E. E. *William McKendree.* Nashville and Dallas: Publishing House of the Methodist Episcopal Church, South, 1914.

Lee, James W., Luccock, Napthali, and Dixon, James M. *The Illustrated History of Methodism.* New York and St. Louis: Methodist Magazine Publishing Co., 1900.

Lee, Leroy M. *Life and Times of Jesse Lee.* Nashville and Dallas: Publishing House of the Methodist Episcopal Church, South, 1848.

McClintock, John (ed.). *Sketches of Eminent Methodist Ministers.* New York: Carlton & Phillips, 1854.

McTyeire, Henry N. *A History of Methodism.* Nashville and Dallas: Publishing House of the Methodist Episcopal Church, South, 1893.

Ruby, R. Carlyle. *The Old Northwest.* Muncie, Indiana: Indiana Historical Society, 1950.

Simpson, Matthew (ed.). *Cyclopaedia of Methodism.* Revised ed. Philadelphia: Louis H. Everts, 1880.

Stevens, Abel. *A Compendious History of American Methodism.* New York: Carlton & Porter, 1867.

Strickland, W. P. (ed.). *Autobiography of James B. Finley.* New York: Eaton & Mains, 1859.

———. *Peter Cartwright, the Backwoods Preacher.* New York and Cincinnati: The Methodist Book Concern, 1856.

Sweet, William Warren (ed.). *The Rise of Methodism in the West.* New York and Cincinnati: The Methodist Book Concern, 1920.

Tipple, Ezra Squire (ed.). *The Heart of Asbury's Journals.* New York: Eaton & Mains, 1904.

Indiana Sources

Brown, Irving Frederick. *Indiana Asbury—DePauw University.* Published as a bulletin of the University in 1914.

Eggleston, Edward (for atmosphere). *The Circuit Rider.* New York: Harper & Bros., 1878.

———. *Hoosier Schoolmaster.* Revised ed. New York: Orange Judd Publishing Co., 1892.

Holliday, Fernandez C. *Indiana Methodism.* Cincinnati: Hitchcock & Walden, 1873.

———. *The Life and Times of Rev. Allen Wiley.* Cincinnati: L. Swormstedt and A. Poe for the Methodist Episcopal Church, 1853.

Johnson, Howard. *A Home in the Woods.* Muncie, Indiana: Indiana Historical Society, 1951.

Nottingham, Elizabeth Kristine. *Methodism and the Frontier.* New York: Columbia University Press, 1941.

Smith, John C. *Reminiscences of Early Methodism in Indiana.* Indianapolis: J. M. Olcott, 1879.

Sweet, William Warren (ed.). *Circuit-rider Days Along the Ohio.* New York and Cincinnati: The Methodist Book Concern, 1923.

———. *Indiana Asbury—DePauw University.* Nashville: Abingdon Press, 1937.

Thompson, R. W. *Fallen Heroes of Indiana Methodism.*

Wood, Aaron. *Annals of the Methodist Episcopal Church in Indiana.* Indiana State Journal Steam Press, 1854.

Woodburn, James Albert. *History of Indiana Uuniversity.* Published by the university, 1940.

Travel Sources

Dunbar, Seymour. *History of Travel in America.* Indianapolis: The Bobbs-Merrill Co., Inc., 1915.

McLean, Nelson. *Memoirs of Gatch.* 1854.

Marshall, John. *Life of Washington.* New York: William H. Wise & Co., 1926.

Also frequent references in books of the period.

Histories of Conferences

Bishop Roberts presided over all the conferences at one time or another, and many times over the earlier conferences. These histories have proved valuable sources of information on Roberts and on the slavery issue.

Arnold, William E. *The History of Methodism in Kentucky.* Vol. I Louisville: Herald Press, 1935-36.

Bennett, William W. *Memorials of Methodism in Virginia.* Richmond: William W. Bennett, 1871.

Grissom, William Lee. *History of Methodism in North Carolina.* Nashville and Dallas: Publishing House of the Methodist Episcopal Church, South, 1905.

Jones, John G. *Methodism in Mississippi,* 2 vols. Nashville: Southern Methodist Publishing House, 1887.

McFerrin, John B. *History of Methodism in Tennessee.* 3 vols. Nashville: Publishing House of the Methodist Episcopal Church, South, 1869-73.

Redford, Albert H. *The History of Methodism in Kentucky.* Vol. III. Nashville: Southern Methodist Publishing House, 1868-70.

Shipp, Albert M. *The History of Methodism in South Carolina.* Nashville: Southern Methodist Publishing House, 1884.

Smith, George G. *History of Methodism in Georgia and Florida.* Macon: J. W. Burke & Co., 1877.

Library and Field Research

Findings of field research appear in the text as background and local traditions. The most helpful libraries have been those at DePauw and Emory universities; the Library of Congress; the archives of the Baltimore Conference at First Church, Baltimore; the historical library of the New York East Conference, 150 Fifth Avenue, New York; W. Lauren Rogers Memorial Library at Laurel, Mississippi; my own library; and that of Edwin W. Dunlavy, New Carlisle, Indiana.

Index